MW00605672

Other Books in the Show Me Missouri Series:

River Valley
COMPANION

A Nature Guide

By Brian Beatte & Brett Dufur
With an introduction by naturalist Randal Clark
Illustrated by Maggie 'Woodwoman' Riesenmy

Pebble Publishing
Columbia, Missouri

Project support by Pebble Publishing staff:
Addie & R.C. Adams, Beckley & Brian Beatte, Tawnee Brown, Brett Dufur,
Daisy Dufur, Jeff Lehman, Pippa Letsky & Hope Wagner

ISBN 0-9646625-1-5 14.95

Pebble Publishing, P.O. Box 431, Columbia, MO 65205-0431
Phone: 1 (800) 576-7322 • Fax: (573) 698-3108
E-Mail: Pebble@showmestate.com
Online: Katytrail.showmestate.com & Trailsidebooks.com

Printed by Ovid Bell Press, Fulton, Missouri, USA

To Warry, a truly "rare critter"
            — Brian

To my river valley companions past and present
            — Brett

Acknowledgments

Many naturalists gave generously of their time and expertise to help see this book through fruition. This three-year project would not have been possible without the help of the following people: Jeanne and Vernon Barr, Carole and John Behrer of the Shaw Arboretum, Vincent Burkes of the Midwest Science Center, Randal Clark of the Midwest Science Center, Jim and Sue Denny, David Diamond (Director, Missouri Resource Assessment Partnership), Joe Engeln, Jean Graebner of the Missouri Audubon Society, Mac Johnson, Marti Kardinal, George Kastler (Chief Parks Naturalist), Dick Luecke of the DNR-DPRHP, Hank Ottinger of Westminster College, Jan Parenteau, Maggie and Robert Riesenmy, Kay Stewart of the Missouri Audubon Society, Jim and Joanne Whitley, and H. Warrington Williams of Westminster College. There are also many others, who have been river valley companions to us, imparting their time-honed knowledge. To all of these teachers, their help in introducing nature to "the rest of us" is gratefully appreciated.

CONTENTS

CONTENTS

PREFACE

How often have you been on a hike and asked, "What's that?" Here's a book to answer many of these questions. This book is a beginner's guide to nature. It includes useful information in a simple, easy-to-understand format. Everything has been researched, reviewed and edited to make nature identification as simple as possible. With over 400 illustrations, this book identifies the Missouri River valley's most common species and explains its diverse ecology, past and present.

The Missouri River valley—often called a basin, the river bottoms and the floodplain—is the region created by the meanders and cutting of the Missouri River. For this book, we limit our scope of the Missouri River valley within the state of Missouri. We define the river valley as all habitats along the Missouri River, from bluff to bluff plus five miles on either side of the floodplain.

Many species found along this valley are also found in other river valley ecosystems, so you will find this book a useful supplement in other areas as well. Beginning naturalists in other Midwestern states would also find this a useful reference.

Many of Missouri's other river valleys—such as the Mississippi, Meramec and Gasconade—also host many of the same species we highlight here. Missouri is bordered by more rivers than any other state. Can you name them all? They include the Missouri River, the Mississippi, the St. Francis, the Osage, the Ohio and the Illinois.

Within the state, the Missouri River travels more than 550 miles from the western slope at the junction of Kansas, Ohio and Missouri to its confluence with the Mississippi River in St. Charles. In addition to the many towns whose original growth was fostered by early river travel, Missouri's two largest cities—St. Louis and Kansas City—continue to thrive along the banks of the Big Muddy.

The Missouri River valley is Missouri's most largely undiscovered gem-in-the-rough. Many naturalists who travel to other states for a respite from the grasp of society would do well to rediscover all that this secluded natural corridor has to offer. It is accessible to more than two-thirds of the state's population in less than one hour, making it the prime place for many Missourians to enjoy nature.

Great places to enjoy the river valley are numerous. One of our favorites is the Katy Trail State Park, which winds over 185 miles from St. Charles to Sedalia. In fact, it's America's longest rails-to-trails project, where an old railroad right-of-way was turned into a gorgeous hiking and biking path. The Katy Trail follows the Missouri River from St. Charles in the east to Boonville in the west before departing from the Missouri River valley and heading southwest to Sedalia.

In addition to the Katy Trail, more than 70 conservation areas, 17 state parks and the Mark Twain National Forest border the Missouri River valley as well as 27 fishing accesses developed by the Department of Conservation. If you are looking for a great place to enjoy nature, you may be closer than you think. We've included seven nature trips and a complete listing of fishing accesses in the back of the book to give you a great start.

This book is very different from other nature guides being published today. On a walk through the woods, many questions often arise. For a long time, if you wanted to learn a little bit more about nature, you would have to arm yourself with at least half a dozen identification guides specializing in different types of plants or animals.

Obviously, these specialized reference books are truly the best way to learn a lot about a certain species or region. Yet, there are many more people who need just a little bit of information, a tidbit of trivia or a river valley companion to allow their interests in nature to flourish. This book was written with these people in mind.

This book is interactive. Once you find something in the wild, check it off your "life list" in the back. This is a handy way to remember what you have seen. Remember too that there are infinite numbers of natural features in the valley, so you are also likely to find something that is not in this book. Also, remember that nature has a way of confounding us with exceptions.

This book, like a good dog, hates being left behind when you go on a hike. The best way to learn more about nature is to get out there and experience it for yourself. Refer to these pages often to learn more about the nature around you. See you there!

BRETT & BRIAN

INTRODUCTION

The great river that gives Missouri its name has been called many things, Nishodse or Muddy Waters, River of the People with Big Canoes, the Big Muddy and the Mighty Mo. Whatever you call it, the Missouri River is undoubtedly one of the great river systems of the world.

The Missouri River is more than 2,300 miles long and drains one sixth of the United States. With its headwaters on the east face of the Rocky Mountains, near Yellowstone National Park, it flows across the Great Plains picking up millions of tons of sediment until it enters the Mississippi River at St. Louis. Beyond St. Louis, the Missouri controls the character of the Mississippi River system to the Gulf of Mexico. There have been strong arguments made that the Mississippi River should even be called a tributary of the Missouri River. If this were so, the Missouri would be the longest river in the world.

As rivers go, the Missouri River is relatively young. A child of the Ice Age, it emerged between 10,000 and 2 million years ago in the wake of the great Continental Glaciers. During this time, each spring and summer would bring wild floods and the river would rush along at the front of the melting glacier. This raging torrent carved the giant valley and massive bluffs that we see today. Eventually, the glaciers retreated to the north, leaving the river to trace their southernmost limits. As the glaciers receded, the landscape as well as the plant and animal communities along the river slowly changed from tundra to the more abundant flora and fauna we now enjoy.

Ten thousand years ago the Missouri River valley was a wild and beautiful thing. It was one of the most biologically productive and diverse places on earth. In the river was an abundant fishery with ancient species of sturgeon, paddlefish, catfish and many others. The river was a placid, braided stream with many channels and sandbars. Periodic flooding allowed the river to meander across its valley constantly creating and destroying channels. This annual process was ideal for wildlife and created great wetland areas that supported abundant waterfowl and shore birds. Great cottonwood forests covered the floodplains. Rich prairies were also found along the floodplain, bordered by immense upland areas. Old growth forests of oak and hickory could be found in these special places. In the forests and prairies could be found many buffalo, elk, deer, bear and a wide variety of other wildlife.

It was during this time that humans first appeared along the Missouri River. In this dynamic region they collected fish and shellfish, hunted great flocks of waterfowl and hunted the abundant wildlife in the forests and prairies. The Woodlands culture of Native Americans lived along the river from the time of Christ to about 1300 A.D. These people were the first to cultivate corn and squash in the fertile floodplain and they built many burial and ceremonial mounds alongside the river. Around 1300 A.D. the Missouri or Niutachi ("People Who Dwell at the Mouth of the River") moved into the area. This tribe lived beside the river at its mouth and in the area around Van Meter State Park. The river was their main source of food and transportation. The Osage, although a tribe that lived mainly in southwest Missouri, also lived with the Missouri tribe for a while near the river.

In the late 1700s Europeans began to trap fur and trade with the Native Americans along the river. The Missouri River was the major route for traders and settlers traveling west. Travel along the river was first by canoe, then keelboat and later steamboat. By 1900, railroads had become the preferred way to travel along beside the river. Towns, then cities, sprang up from east to west. Most of the bottomland forests, prairies and wetlands were quickly converted to cornfields. The Missouri River endured another series of massive changes after World War II when the upper part of the river was dammed to form lakes. For these dams, 755 miles of the cottonwood forest went under water. Along the lower part of the river from Sioux City downstream, the river was developed for navigation. The river was cleared, dredged, narrowed and straightened. The backwaters and oxbow lakes and marshes were filled with accumulated silt.

The impact of these dramatic changes has forever changed the Missouri River valley. The majority of backwater spawning and nursery areas for fish are today just a memory. Most of the sandbars used by shore birds have disappeared. Thousands of areas of lush bottomland forests, marshes and prairies used by the waterfowl and wildlife have been destroyed. In the last 100 years alone there has been a 50–90 percent decrease in many of the habitats along the river—the same habitats that support thousands of species of plants and animals. The buffalo, elk, wolf and bear were the first species to disappear. Several species of birds have disappeared as well and many others have become endangered. As the changes continue, many of the river's fish may soon follow. Recently, the Missouri River was declared one of the most threatened in the United States.

There is hope. Several conservation agencies are working on setting land aside and letting the river reclaim its ancient floodplain. We may never go back to the natural ecosystem of 200 years ago, but for the sake of our descendants we must manage the river valley so that we maintain and enhance the current biological diversity.

This is one of the first books to cover the entire natural history of the Missouri River valley. With the help of this book, you will be introduced to the natural history of one of the great river valleys of the world. It is my hope that you will have fun gaining a greater understanding of this special river valley and the abundance of natural features that it supports.

RANDAL CLARK

NATURALIST

Remember ...

If one looks hard enough, and walks far enough, he will still find wild places. Places where solitude breathes. They are tucked between mans reflections of progress. Forgotten roadways and valleys still intact — small creek beds and bends of rivers, along jagged bluff lines and soils too poor for farming.
These places, between massaged fields and channelized rivers remain.
Stay attuned for these signs of forgottenness, for these places, like a warm December day, are fleeting ...

How to Use This Book

A t the beginning of each section, there is an introduction, a sample entry and an outline to help you get started. Take a minute to familiarize yourself with the book's organization and find out how it can help you learn more about the natural world. For example, wildflowers are organized first by color then by season.

Let your experiences guide you. While observing nature, consult this book's index, page headers and tabs to quickly locate your new discoveries. Once you answer "What's that?" jot yourself a few notes for easier identification next time. We've left ample room on each page for you to make notes. There are also several blank pages in the back of this book for longer notes and sketches.

A Disclaimer about Wild Edibles!

A fter considerable deliberation, we decided to include a limited amount of information about commonly seen edible plants, fruits and berries. Remember that it is against the rules in most public nature areas to pick, gather or consume wild plants. In addition to the potentially serious effects that can result from eating an incorrectly identified plant, many edibles, like those along the Katy Trail State Park, have been treated with herbicides. So even the edible ones may give you problems!

So why did we include this information? Knowing the natural history of a certain plant often gives you a greater understanding of how a certain species fits into the continually evolving relationship between man and nature. Exposure to this information in and of itself cannot harm you.

There are four major landscapes in the Missouri River Valley:

FLOODPLAINS,

MISSOURI RIVER HILLS,

OZARK BORDER &

OSAGE PLAINS

The Missouri River divides the Glacial Plains (North) from the Ozark Highlands (South) and the Western Plains (South). These major divisions define the borders of the Missouri River Valley.

Immersion in Nature

A common question is, "What is the best way for me to see as many species as possible?"

While some nature buffs prefer to hike long distances, some of the most rewarding experiences in the outdoors come from sitting still. You will only notice as much as you allow yourself to notice, whether by hiking all day or sitting all day. The latter requires attention, silence and patience.

Many of nature's displays are so small that they are easily overlooked unless you stop and look closely. Many times, sitting still in one spot allows you to fully enjoy all of nature's sights, sounds and smells. Many birds actually become more vocal the longer you sit still. In addition to bird songs, the keen observer will be surprised by an amazing number of busy creatures, many so hard at work they may not even notice your quiet observations.

The limestone rock that abounds in this region is another perfect example. Though at a distance it appears as a single mass, upon closer examination, you realize that limestone is comprised of millions of fossils packed together by seas millions of years ago.

Below are nine easy ways to acquaint yourself with the natural world:

1. Find a favorite spot and return to it at different times and seasons

2. Listen to the bird songs (best at sunrise and sunset)

3. Look for tracks, identify what made them and then try to figure out what they were doing

4. Draw or write what you see on the blank pages of this book

5. Trace leaves or make rubbings of fossils you find embedded in limestone

6. Examine and smell flowers, leaving them intact for the next nature lover

7. Limit your observations to just a small part of the landscape and see how many of its features you can notice

8. Watch the sky and count the many groups of birds, butterflies and insects

9. Study the many creatures busy at work in the first two inches of soil

THE WELL-DRESSED HIKER

- ❏ Comfortable clothes (layered during fall, winter and spring)
- ❏ Sturdy shoes
- ❏ Hat to keep you shaded
- ❏ Water
- ❏ G.O.R.P. "Good Old Raisins and Peanuts"
- ❏ A trail guide or map
- ❏ Pencil and small pad for drawing or writing
- ❏ Sunglasses
- ❏ Sunscreen
- ❏ Compass
- ❏ Small calculator
- ❏ Magnifying glass
- ❏ Flashlight
- ❏ Insect repellent
- ❏ Binoculars
- ❏ Small camera
- ❏ Band-Aids
- ❏ Small trash bag for picking up litter
- ❏ Other things I should bring: _____

Rules That Apply to Conservation Areas & Private Lands

The following rules should be kept in mind when you are enjoying public areas. Remember to leave an area even better than you found it. Also, you should always get permission before exploring on private land. If you receive permission, avoid damaging the landowner's property and say "thank you" on your way out.

Although this list is not definitive (many areas have special rules) it is a good place to start:

- No littering.
- No fireworks.
- No open fires.
- No free-running pets. Dogs must be leashed.
- Motor vehicles restricted to parking areas and roadways.
- Destroying, cutting or removing vegetation is prohibited.
- Nuts, berries, fruits, mushrooms and wild greens may be taken for personal consumption only. Taking of wild greens from designated natural areas, in any amount, is not allowed.
- No target shooting allowed.
- Swimming is prohibited.
- No hunting from levees or roads.

READING THE "MIGHTY MO"

Many people have said, "The Missouri River—It's too thick to drink and too thin to plow." The Big Muddy, as it is often called, drains one-sixth of the entire United States, carrying large quantities of silt downriver in the process.

Its color changes from deep chocolate brown to blue to green, depending upon the season and rainfall. As the river rises, it picks up more sediment and becomes a deeper brown. Each year it carries more than 350,000,000 tons of sand and silt to its confluence, or meeting point, with the Mississippi River near St. Louis. The two rivers then flow south as one to the Gulf of Mexico.

Nature is a dynamic force that changes much like a person does as they grow up. The Missouri River valley has undergone many changes as it has aged. The river was not always a swift, single body of water. In fact, when Lewis and Clark ventured up the Missouri River in 1804, they encountered a river very different from today.

Two hundred years ago, the river was a series of braided channels that constantly moved, as sand bars and eroding banks made the river an ever-changing landscape. Bank to bank, the river stretched close to a mile wide at times. It was more like a slow-moving wetland than a single river channel.

These vast wetlands supported a wide variety of wildlife in numbers that are almost unimaginable today. For the past 100 years, the Corps of Engineers has implemented its Master Plan for the Missouri River, which has channelized and stabilized the river's meandering tendencies and has strengthened many eroding banks. The majority of the original wetland areas and oxbow lakes have been eliminated by these changes. In fact, in the past 100 years, the Missouri River has been shortened 46 miles by the combined acts of man and nature.

Although the "Mighty Mo" will continue to evolve, it will always remain a fundamental and defining resource of the region. The following list of terms will provide you with a useful introduction to some of the features of the river.

Although this book is a great river valley companion, nothing should replace going with a good friend. The Missouri River is a powerful river, with an average current of 8-12 miles an hour. Extreme care should be taken when enjoying it and the abundant nature around it. Because of the strong current and undertow, swimming, wading and getting too close can be deadly.

Face Downstream for 'River Right'

Correct orientation is important. Several other river terms depend on this point of reference so just remember that if you are facing downstream, 'river right is your right' and 'river left is your natural left.'

Left Bank & Right Bank

To determine the left and right banks, face downstream—the left bank is now on your left and the right bank is on your right.

Bends & Meanders

These are the large S-shaped curves all along the Missouri River. A bend, or meander, in the river usually indicates that the river's path has been altered by some geologic feature. Even rivers in flat areas will form bends as they try to reach sea level. They will meander more and more as the land around them flattens out. Since the Missouri River is between 500 and 1,000 feet elevation within the state of Missouri, it has formed many bends. Rivers in the Rocky Mountains, however, develop very straight channels, as the water rushes steeply down to reach sea level.

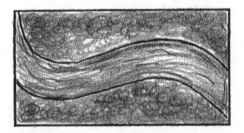

Reaches

A reach is the long, straight section of river between bends.

Boils

Boils occur when fast moving water pours over a sand dune on the river bottom. When the fast moving current pours over the peak of one dune and into the trough of another, the water crashes with such force that it climbs the face of the next dune and disrupts the river's surface.

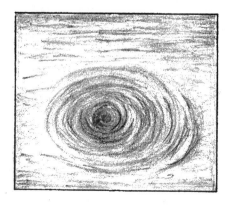

Whirlpools

These turbulent, spinning features are created by standing obstructions in the river's path. When water flows against these obstacles, it is deflected and results in a churning surface. Points of land and large masses of river debris can produce powerful whirlpools.

Navigation Buoys

Red and black buoys are used to mark the navigation channel. Red buoys are called "nuns" and are on the left side of the channel as you face downstream. Black buoys, or "cans," are on the right side of the channel. A boat moving downstream in the channel would therefore pass to the right of a "nun" and to the left of a "can." In addition to helping barges and other boats stay in the main channel, buoys are used to mark obstructions and other danger areas.

Levees & Dikes

Levees are man-made embankments used to prevent flooding in lowlands bordering the river. Dikes maintain the channel and flow of the river. Constructed of rocks and pilings, dikes preserve the main channel (prevent it from being filled in) and protect the river's banks from erosion.

Levee

Dike

Floodplain

The floodplain includes any lowlands that represent the past, present or future course of the river. The floodplain also includes any bordering lands that may be affected by the rise and fall of the river's channel.

Riprap

Rock used to construct and maintain shoreline, revetments, dikes and levees. The rock slows erosion of soft soils.

Oxbow Lakes

These are created when bends in the river are cut off from the main channel, primarily due to flooding. This creates marshes covered with Cat-Tails and other wetland grasses. These marshes, like wetlands, are the most useful form of habitat for many plant and animal species. Over time, these oxbow lakes can become separated from the river by miles. These lakes are quite a sight to see from the air.

Blue Hole Lakes

These were created by floodwaters that scoured into an area, quickly eroding the soil and creating a lake sometimes 100 feet deep. As the floodwaters recede, these "blue holes" remain—bright blue and teeming with fish—cut off from the main channel until the next flood. Interestingly enough, though the blue hole and the river appear disconnected at the surface, when the river rises, the surface of the blue hole lake rises as well.

Tributary Streams

The many creeks and tributaries that empty into the Missouri River are important arteries that drain the nearby landscape and contribute to the main channel's massive volume of water. Some of these tributaries include the Auxvasse, Perche, Wakenda and Kansas.

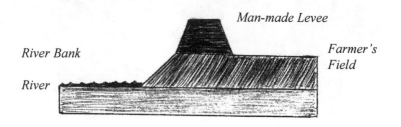

Man-made Levee

River Bank

Farmer's Field

River

TYPES OF NATURAL COMMUNITIES

There are many different types of natural communities that you will likely encounter as you explore. The diverse natural environments have been illustrated here to introduce you to the prominent features of this region.

The most commonly seen natural communities are:

CLIFFS

FOREST

PRAIRIE

Savanna

Farm
Fields

Wetlands

Rocks, Soils & Fossils

Limestone is the most commonly seen rock along the river valley. The majority of what you will encounter is Burlington limestone, formed from 95 percent calcium carbonate. It contains many fossil fragments, such as crinoids, brachiopods and corals.

Geologists have named the different layers, generally from the town closest to the surface layers. Burlington limestone, which is what you see near Rocheport, was named for Burlington, Iowa. It is particularly rich in brachiopods and crinoid fossils. The Cooper-Callaway layer contains many species of coral. There is an outcrop of St. Peters sandstone, that is made of pure white sand, on the east side of the Loutre River. It is easy to see from I-70 and visible along the eastern edges of the Katy Trail from Rocheport to St. Charles.

The movement
of the river
helps to grind
and smooth rocks

Boulders larger than 8 in.
Cobbles from 2 to 8 in.
Pebbles from 3/8 to 2 in.
Gravel from 1/8 to 3/8 in.
Sand from 1/250 to 1/8 in.
Silt from 1/2500 to 1/25 in.
Clay less than 1/2500 in.

Another common rock is chert. Chert is also called jasper, flint and mozarkite. Chert is composed entirely of silica. You will find it deposited among layers of limestone and dolomite as lumps or nodules. Chert often feels smooth like glass and tends to break with sharp edges. Native Americans used the best quality chert to make their arrowheads, scraping tools and knives.

Chert was formed by direct crystallization of silica from minerals found in warm, shallow seas that covered Missouri in ancient times. Organic matter falling to the ocean floor was also replaced with silica. Many fossils were preserved this way.

Missouri's state rock, mozarkite, is a colorful type of chert. It has lots of red and pink coloring mixed with the usual white, grey, black, brown and yellow. Mozarkite is often polished and made into jewelry.

Beneath these commonly seen layers of limestone and chert are massive amounts of precambrian igneous rock created one to two billion years ago by lava flows. These older layers are best seen at Elephant Rocks State Park in southeastern Missouri.

In addition to native stones, you are likely to find a few unusual rocks. Twenty different kinds of rock have been found in the Missouri River sands. These rocks roll and tumble downriver as a result of erosion and excavation of glacial deposits by the river's unyielding flow. Small pieces of petrified wood, agate, quartz, fossils of sea creatures and occasionally animal bones can also often be found on the river's sandbars. Many of these are called glacial erratics and were deposited here by ancient glaciers.

Not all rocks are carried into this area by the Missouri River. The railroad beds were constructed with cobbles and boulders of rock more durable than limestone. Many of these rocks came from the southeastern Taum Sauk area, which has hard, volcanic rock. Our state mineral—galena, or lead ore—also comes from this southeastern region.

Soils

Soil is the result of the weathering of rocks and the decay of plant and animal materials. Usually the wide river bottoms have a black, sticky soil called gumbo. It is made up of fine silt, clay and decaying plant matter. When floodwaters rise slowly, the silt, clay and organic particles have time to settle, enriching the soil and making the bottomland soil many times more fertile than soils on nearby hilltops. Swifter flood currents deposit heavier weight particles, such as sand, onto the bottomlands.

In addition to gumbo soil, the river valley is also known for its loess soil, which is comprised of clay and fine sand. The loess soil was deposited by melt water rivers as the glaciers receded from Missouri during the Ice Age. The loess soil was carried by the wind and eventually deposited in Missouri resulting in the filling of a large portion of the Missouri River floodplain.

Fossils
Remnants of Past Seas

The whole interior of the United States from the Rocky Mountains to the Appalachian Mountains was a great sea for millions of years. The sea from 570 to 225 million years ago, during the Paleozoic Era, deposited nearly all of the rock that underlies today's Missouri. More than 8,000 feet of rock was deposited during this period. This was primarily limestone inlaid with shale and sandstone. This sedimentary rock settled in layers from these ancient waters, now easily visible in the bluffs that line much of the Missouri River valley.

Due to continental drift, Missouri was once much closer to the Equator. During this period, the land rose above and fell below sea level many times, and was covered by warm, shallow seas many times. During the Mississippian period, 325 million years ago, the majority of the limestone was deposited. Brachiopods and crinoids were extremely numerous. Finally, 280 million years ago, the Missouri area emerged from the seas for the last recorded time.

Along the eastern section of the Katy Trail State Park, from Boone County to St. Louis, St. Peter sandstone is found, though not as frequently as dolomite limestone. St. Peter sandstone is the purest silica sandstone in the world and is used for making fine glassware and high-quality optics.

Commonly Found Missouri Fossils

Crinoids (sea lilies)
This is Missouri's state fossil

Gastropods
(early snail-like form)

TRILOBITES

CORALS

PLANT FOSSILS

BLASTOIDS

BRYOZOANS
(MOSS ANIMALS)

BRACHIOPODS
(LAMP SHELLS)

WHEN YOU FIND YOUR FIRST FOSSIL...

... MAKE A RUBBING OF IT HERE

TREES &
SHRUBS

What is the difference? A fully grown tree usually stands taller than 17 feet from a single base stem. A shrub has several stems growing from its base and is usually smaller. But to complicate matters, some trees take the form of shrubs in inhospitable environments. Since the shape of a tree is greatly affected by its distance from other trees, it is better to use leaves for identification rather than tree shapes, since a tree in an open field will grow differently than a tree in a closely knit forest.

Trees are divided into hardwoods and softwoods. Hardwoods grow slowly and the wood is very dense, making the trees solid and durable. The most common hardwood trees are oaks and hickories. Silver maple, black walnut, bur oak and sycamore are also frequently seen.

Softwoods include the conifers, such as pine trees, which are green all year with needle-like leaves and seeds contained in some type of cone. In Missouri there are only two species of native softwoods: the Eastern Red Cedar and the Short-Leaf Pine. Therefore, the majority of trees you are likely to encounter will be hardwood varieties.

Bottomland forests provide food and cover for many species. Though in the early 1800s extensive forests and prairies covered much of the floodplain, they have been reduced in most areas today to increase usable farmland for growing corn, wheat, milo and soybeans.

Fall Colors

Throughout autumn, brilliant fall leaves blanket the river valley. Have you ever wondered what makes the leaves change colors? The red, yellow and orange colors are the result of a chemical process. During the spring and summer months, chlorophyll (contained in food storage structures called chloroplasts) is responsible for the green colors that we see. As cooler temperatures set in, the chlorophyll is used by the trees for nourishment, which also removes the green color of the leaf. The leaves eventually wither, turning rich golds, browns and reds, and finally fall to the ground.

Chloroplasts, in addition to containing chlorophyll, retain pigments called carotenoids. Carotenoids begin to affect leaf colors in the fall, as the amount of chlorophyll begins to decline during the cooler and shorter days of autumn. The now more abundant carotenoid pigments yield the yellow and orange colors that adorn many of the hardwood trees, including hickory, maple, cottonwood and sassafras. Some species, such as the oaks, display red or orange tints in the early spring. Their colorful presentation is due to the large amounts of carotenoids contained in the leaves that have not yet been masked by chlorophyll.

Other pigments called anthocyanins produce the purples and reds. Unlike chlorophyll, anthocyanins are not present in the leaves during the spring and summer growing season. Instead, these pigments develop late in the summer and occur only in the sap of the leaf cells. The brilliant purple and red hues produced by these pigments are prominent in oaks, maples, sweetgums and dogwood.

The combination of chlorophyll, carotenoids and anthocyanins often yield a spectacular display of fall colors. Although these processes are linked to the fall weather patterns that vary from year to year, trees in the Missouri River valley typically display their brightest colors during a six-week period from the middle of September to late October, with the height of their variety and brilliance occurring in mid-October.

A Sample Entry for Trees and Shrubs

COMMON NAME
Scientific Name
Size: Average height of mature tree or shrub.
Description: General features, bark characteristics and color.
Leaves: Description of leaf shapes. Includes flowers, fruits and acorns if present.
Where to find: Soil preferences and distribution.
Note: May include other local names, interesting facts or trivia.

MAKING LEAF PRINTS
& BARK RUBBINGS

P art of the fun of exploring is preserving the nature you encounter. Journal entries, sketches and photographs are great ways to record your experiences while also preserving nature for others. Making leaf prints and bark rubbings is a low impact, fun way to learn more about trees and shrubs.

LEAF PRINTS

Materials: Printers ink, rubber roller, smooth pane of glass (Plexiglass can also be used and is great because it won't break), a rolling pin, paper and tweezers.

Instructions:

1) Place a small amount of water-based ink on the glass.
2) Roll the ink out evenly with the rubber roller.
3) Place the leaf on the ink-covered glass.
4) Roll the ink-covered roller over the surface of the leaf not exposed to the glass.
5) Now pick up the inked leaf with your tweezers and place it on a sheet of paper.
6) Place another sheet of paper on top of the leaf.
7) Now, run the rolling pin over the paper-leaf-paper assembly.

Water and towels can be used for easy cleanup.
These beautiful prints can then be preserved in a binder, labeled and combined with notes from your outing.

BARK RUBBINGS

Materials: Waxed paper and a crayon.

Instructions: Hold or tape a piece of waxed paper against the bark. Take a crayon and rub it on the waxed paper. Rub the crayon firmly enough to transfer the bark pattern, but be careful not to tear the paper.

WHITE ASH
Fraxinus americana
Fall Colors: Gold, purple or bronze.
Size: Up to 120 ft.
Description: Ashy gray to brown bark, deeply divided by narrow ridges. Older trees bear diamond-shaped ridges. Opposite branching.
Leaves: From 8 to 12 in. with 5–9 (usually 7) oblong leaflets, each 3–5 in. long. Smooth or finely toothed. Fruits grow in crowded clusters. Male and female flowers are borne on separate trees. Flowers from April to May.
Where to find: A forest tree needing rich, moist soil, often found with oaks, hickories and maples. This familiar tree loves light and is unknown to heavily shaded areas. Commonly found along the edges of major rivers and streams. In fact, this tree can be found in every county along the Missouri River.
Note: Wood is used for baseball bats and oars, as well as furniture and cabinets.

The **white ash** is known for its favorable burning characteristics. The wood of young saplings can also be shaved to use as kindling to start a fire.

BASSWOOD
Tilia americana
Fall Colors: Pale green to pale yellow.
Size: Up to 80 ft.
Description: Handsome shade tree with ridged and furrowed, light brown bark. Likes space.
Leaves: From 5 to 6 in., heart-shaped. Deeply veined and fine-toothed. Base of leaf uneven. Has yellow flowers in spring, which hang on fragrant strips.
Where to find: Rich soils and bottomlands.
Note: Also called the Linden Tree. Its light wood is prized by carvers for its fine, even grain. Its flowers are very fragrant and are an important source of honey.

The name of this tree comes from "bass" or bast, which refers to the tree's inner wood. Although today it is primarily used by woodworkers, the tree was used in earlier times to produce a natural fiber that was woven to create a wide variety of items. This natural fiber was generated by crushing strips of **basswood** bark.

SILVER MAPLE
Acer saccharinum
Fall Colors: Pale yellow.
Size: Up to 80 ft.
Description: Bark is smooth and light gray. In older trees, the bark is thin and scaly.
Leaves: From 6 to 7 in. wide, light green above, silver below, 5 double-toothed, lobed, opposite. Two joined seeds with wings at right angles, widely spread.
Where to find: Prefers moist sites such as low-lying river and stream valleys.
Note: Although its colors are not nearly as impressive as those of the Sugar Maple, it is an extremely popular ornamental tree because it grows fast.

The common name of this beautiful tree comes from the two-toned leaves that it produces. While the tops of its leaves present a pale green color, the undersides have a distinctive silvery-white appearance. The gentle winds of summer, combined with sunlight, often produce a sparkling effect. Also, just prior to a storm, when the wind is really blowing, the leaves on the **silver maple** turn upside down and show their paler side. This is when old-timers would often say, "Its petticoat is showing!"

SUGAR MAPLE
Acer saccharum
Fall Colors: Brilliant red, orange and yellow.
Size: Up to 80 ft.
Description: Thick, light gray to brown bark. Vertical furrows and plate-like scales.
Leaves: From 4 to 5 in. wide, 5 lobed, veined, bright green leaves, with sparse, large pointed teeth. Rounded on bottom. The two joined seeds are parallel.
Where to find: Rich, moist soils.
Note: Brilliantly red, orange and yellow in the fall.

The sap of the **sugar maple** is used to produce fine maple syrups. The sap contains approximately 2 percent sugar and is naturally sweet. As much as 40 gallons of sap are needed to produce 1 gallon of syrup.

COTTONWOOD

Populus deltoides

Fall Colors: Greenish-yellow to dull yellow.

Size: Up to 100 ft.

Description: Fast-growing. Young tree bark is smooth and greenish. The bark of older trees is dark gray and heavily furrowed.

Leaves: From 3 to 6 in., veined, triangle-shaped with coarse rounded teeth. Fruit capsule is green with cottony seeds.

Where to find: Floodplains. Common to bottomlands along streams and rivers.

Note: Used by Native Americans to make long boats for use on the Pekitanoui (or River of the Big Canoes, as the Missouri River was originally called).

Although its wood is white, the tree's name comes from the cotton-like material where its seeds are found. These cotton-like seeds fill the air in June. When stirred by a summer breeze, the leaves of the **cottonwood** generate a pleasant rustling sound.

RED CEDAR

Juniperus virginiana

Fall Colors: Evergreen.

Size: Up to 50 ft.

Description: Bark is peeling red brown.

Leaves: Evergreen, sharp, thin, needle-like overlapping leaves. Scale-like when mature but needle-like when young. Dark blue fruit. Deep green in summer. Winter coloration (depending on exposure) can vary from copper yellow to rusty brown.

Where to find: Woods, rocky slopes, limestone bluffs, old fields, pastures and fencerows.

Note: Wood is used to make pencils, to line cedar chests and make outdoor furniture. Its berries are used to flavor gin.

Known to the French as *baton rouge* (red stick), the hardy and pleasant-smelling **red cedar** is very common. Another name, Graveyard Tree, comes from Ozark lore, which says that when a cedar that you planted grows high enough to shade your grave you will die. Its scent naturally repels moths. The berries of female cedars provide food for songbirds in the winter and many birds make their nests in cedars. Deer also browse on these trees in the winter, and bucks often rub their antlers against smaller cedars. This tree depends on birds, since its seeds must pass through a bird's digestive tract before they will germinate.

BLACK WALNUT
Juglans nigra
Fall Colors: Light yellow.
Size: Up to 80 ft.

Description: Bark is deep gray-brown and furrowed.
Leaves: Alternate, 12–24 in. with 15–23 sharply oval, toothed, long pointed leaflets, approximately 3 in. each. Fruit is borne singly or in pairs, is round and covered with a thick green fibrous husk. The nut has irregular ridges and is oval to oblong. Good to eat. Has a distinctive flavor. Be aware that the husks can stain hands and clothing!
Where to find: Deep moist soils, such as creek bottoms, floodplains or at the base of protected slopes.
Note: Some of Missouri's most prized wood. Most goes into furniture and gunstocks.

The **black walnut** most often grows alone, scattered throughout the forest or in small groves. This growth pattern is due in part to the fact that its roots produce a growth-inhibiting chemical that impedes the growth of other plants, trees and even other walnut trees from growing too near, which could deplete soil nutrients and compete for sunlight.

PECAN
Carya illinoensis
Fall Colors: Golden yellow-brown.
Size: Up to 100 ft.

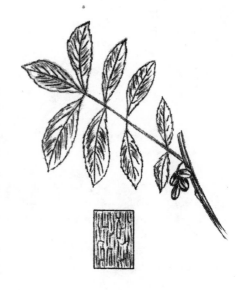

Description: Dark reddish-brown bark, deeply furrowed. Spreading crown if space allows. Twigs are hairy.
Leaves: Alternate, 12–20 in. long, with 9–17 lance-shaped, finely toothed leaflets. Brown thin-shelled nuts grow in clusters of 3–12 and are smooth and oblong. Good to eat.
Where to find: Bottomlands, typically located on cool and protected slopes.
Note: Pecan nuts are just as popular with wildlife as they are with humans.

SHAGBARK HICKORY
Carya ovata
Fall Colors: Yellow.
Size: Up to 80 ft.
Description: Bark is light gray and separates into plates.
Leaves: Compound with 5 leaflets, finely toothed and sharply pointed. The nut grows to 1–2 in. diameter and is surrounded by a husk—the nut within is sweet and good to eat.
Where to find: Prefers deep, moist soil. Grows rapidly in the bottomlands but is also found throughout upland areas.
Note: The tough and resilient wood is used to fashion implement handles and sporting goods. Hickory is also a favorite with barbecuers, who prize the flavor its aroma adds to their culinary creations. These tough trees are an important source of food for many animals.

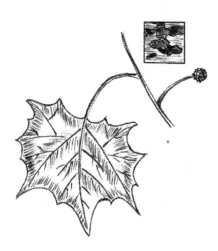

SYCAMORE
Platanus occidentalis
Fall Colors: Brown to tan.
Size: Up to 80 ft.
Description: Bark is dark brown, with scales on the upper trunk, exposing a cream-colored layer underneath. The fruit is rough, bristly and ball-shaped. Are known to grow the greatest trunk diameters of North American hardwood trees—up to 16 feet.
Leaves: Wide, almost heart-shaped, large toothed, with 3–5 shallow lobes.
Where to find: Floodplains in rich moist soil and along stream banks.
Note: Often called the Ghost Tree because of exposed cream-colored bark. You know a spring or creek is nearby when you see the sycamore tree.

The **sycamore** can become gigantic. In the early 1800s, a young attorney who eventually became a St. Louis Circuit Court judge, Nathaniel Tucker, made his home in a Missouri sycamore that had a diameter of 8 ft. (width of the largest sycamore found in Missouri). After cutting the tree to 10 feet above its base, he cleaned the stump out, installed a door and filled it with his law books. He resided and practiced law in this unique house for many years, which, unfortunately, no longer remains.

HONEY LOCUST
Gleditsia triacanthos
Fall Colors: Clear yellow.
Size: Up to 80 ft.
Description: Branches and trunk have many 3-forked thorns that may grow to be as large as 7 in. long. Crown of tree is flat-topped and broad. Bark is gray or dark brown and divides into narrow flat plates.
Leaves: From 7 to 8 in. long, with as many as 28 leaflets, 1–1 1/2 in. long. They are oval, shiny and dark green above, with a lighter dull green underneath. They have a dark brown pod, 12–18 in. long, which contains oval seeds. Pods are prized by dried-flower arrangers and tend to twist into corkscrew shapes before they fall.
Where to find: Likes moist bottomlands but can also grow in dry sites.
Note: Thorns were used by settlers and natives for pins and even spearpoints. Named for the sweet-tasting fiber around each seed.

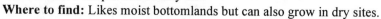
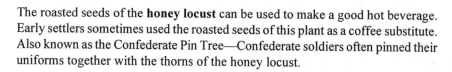

The roasted seeds of the **honey locust** can be used to make a good hot beverage. Early settlers sometimes used the roasted seeds of this plant as a coffee substitute. Also known as the Confederate Pin Tree—Confederate soldiers often pinned their uniforms together with the thorns of the honey locust.

BLACK LOCUST
Robinia pseudoacacia
Fall Colors: Slight yellow-green.
Size: Up to 80 ft.
Description: Tall, thin and very straight. Twigs bear sharp thorns from 1/2 to 1 in. long at leaf base. Brown bark and its heavy ridges give it a rope-like appearance.
Leaves: Each compound leaf is 8–14 in. long and made up of 7–19 thin, smooth oval leaflets that alternate on the stem. The flowers that hang in long clusters like grapes are exceptionally fragrant and bloom in May. Fruit forms flat brown pods, which generally persist through the winter.
Where to find: Grows in a variety of soils, but likes rich, moist limestone soils.
Note: This hardwood can last almost a century without rotting. The leaves of the **black locust** "sleep" at night—each leaflet folds upon the primary stem.

OSAGE ORANGE
Maclura pomifera

Fall Colors: Orange to greenish-yellow.

Size: Up to 40 ft.

Description: Very thorny tree. The bark is dark orange-colored, thick and deeply furrowed.

Leaves: Are dark green, pointed and oval, smooth margined and come to a point. The greenish-yellow fruit grows from a ball of small green flowers and ripens in the fall. Each fruit is 4–5 in. in diameter, rough-surfaced and filled with a thick milky juice.

Where to find: Floodplains and hedgerows.

Note: Native Americans prized the wood for bows and war clubs as it is exceptionally strong and hard, but flexible. Settlers used it for fence posts and to create "living" fencerows.

Named for the orange-like fruit that it produces, the **Osage orange** was first called *bois d'arc* or "bow wood" by the French. This valuable tree, which produces some of the most durable wood cultivated from Missouri's forests, originally shared the same geographical distribution as the early Native American Osage tribe. In addition to its flexible and durable wood, the bark of the Osage orange roots produces a yellow dye, which was used in early textile production.

WILD CRAB
Pyrus coronaria

Size: Up to 30 ft.

Description: Branches have thorn-like spurs. Reddish-brown with thin, cracked scales.

Leaves: Alternate, egg-shaped to oblong, irregular and coarsely toothed. Flowers are in clusters of 3–6 and bloom in April and May. Each flower has 5 petals, which range in color from white to deep rose pink.

Where to find: Old fields, edges of woods and along streams. Seeds are often carried and deposited in the excrement of animals. Also called the Garlandtree.

HAWTHORN
Crataegus pruinosa
Fall Colors: Dull orange to red.
Size: Up to 12 ft.
Description: Shrub-like and thorny with scaly, gray bark.
Leaves: Alternate, dark green, irregular with sharp teeth, some egg-shaped. Flowers are in white clusters with 5 petals on each flower. Blooms in April and May.
Where to find: Rocky areas and abandoned fields.
Note: Planted as fences by early settlers. Many species in Missouri and they almost all have thorns.

The **hawthorn** is Missouri's state flower. Although there are nearly 100 species of this member of the rose family in the state, the distinctions are usually subtle and many of these species lack common names. In addition to the protective shelter that it provides birds, the hawthorn produces a fruit that birds, small animals and even deer use to supplement their winter diets. The fruit ripens in late fall and is similar in appearance to a small crabapple.

WILD PLUM
Prunus americana
Fall Colors: Pale golden yellow.
Size: Up to 20 ft.
Description: Can be shrub-like or a small tree. Dark, reddish-brown bark forms thick plates when trees mature.
Leaves: Long pointed, sharp-toothed, alternate. Flowers are white with 5 petals clustered close to branches (they do not have a pleasant odor). Blooms in April and May. Fruit comes in October as a red ball approximately 1 in. Sweet when fully ripe, but you had better beat the birds.
Where to find: Bottomlands, hedgerows and edges of streams.
Note: Makes a good jam.

PERSIMMON
Diospyros virginiana
Fall Colors: Soft burgundy.
Size: Up to 80 ft.
Description: This is a slender tree, most grow to be much smaller than 80 ft. Male and female trees. Only the female trees bear fruit. Bark is dark brown and broken into blocks in mature trees.
Leaves: Oval, 2–6 in., shiny dark green and alternate. Fruit is purple-orange when ripe. Is not typically palatable until after the first frost.
Where to find: Bottomlands, hedgerows and borders of old fields.
Note: The heavy, dense wood is used for many sporting goods, most notably the construction of golf club heads. The persimmon was a staple in the diet of Native Americans.

Although many people enjoy the taste of the **persimmon** fruit, some will find it harsh and bitter—this is a common reaction when the fruit is eaten before it is ripe. (The fruit is ripe when the stem comes of easily.) The Native American Osage combined the fruit with ground corn to make a bread called stancia. For birds and small animals the persimmon is an important source of food—the fruit being a favorite of the opossum.

RED MULBERRY
Morus rubra
Fall Colors: Golden yellow.
Size: Up to 50 ft.
Description: Bark is dark brown with a reddish tinge and scaly.
Leaves: Alternate, heart-shaped or lobed with small blunt teeth, hairy underneath and rough. Leaves and twigs yield a milky juice. Fruits look like small blackberries and appear in midsummer. Red when immature, turning black when ripe. They are edible.
Where to find: Bottomlands and moist soil.
Note: Almost always an understory tree and has very attractive horizontal branching.

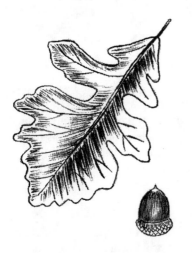

Missouri's Oaks

Missouri oaks are typically divided into the white oaks and the red oaks. The genus *Quercus* includes over 20 different species throughout the state. The variety of oaks is a result of their natural ability to produce viable hybrids. Hybridization often produces characteristics that make it hard to correctly identify a particular oak. These spectacular trees make many contributions to the character of our native forests and to the wildlife that make their homes there.

BUR OAK

Quercus macrocarpa

Fall Colors: Yellow.

Size: Up to 100 ft.

Description: One of the most drought resistant oaks. Thick spreading branches, grayish-brown deep vertical ridged bark, irregular rounded crown.

Leaves: Long 6—12 in., wide 3—6 in., with deep indentations near center. Wedge-shaped, largest at the top. Each leaf is rounded, divided into lobes, 5–7 in. Acorn is large, up to 1 1/2 in. long, scaled with hairy fringe.

Where to find: Prefers moist soil, but can also occur in poor, dry soil in fields and along roadsides.

Note: The Williamson Bur Oak, a 350-year-old tree, can be seen south of Huntsdale, in western Boone County, near the Katy Trail.

The name Mossy-Cup is a common name that is given to the **bur oak**. The name comes from the acorns that the tree produces. It can be identified by the mossy growth of elongated scales that are present on the edge of the acorn. It is known to bear the largest leaves and acorns of all the oaks.

PIN OAK
Quercus palustris
Fall Colors: Bronze or red.
Size: Up to 70 ft.
Description: Named for the many short, pin-like twigs along the horizontal or downward sloping branches. Bark is grayish-brown.
Leaves: Dark shiny, 4–6 in., with 5–7 deeply divided, toothed and sharply pointed lobes. Ends of each lobe has 2–3 divisions, each bristle tipped. Acorn is round, small, about 1/2 in., light brown with a thin, scaly, saucer-shaped cup.
Where to find: Likes moist soil along streams and in valleys. Often used as an ornamental tree.

The **pin oak** is admired for its dazzling fall foliage. In addition to its beauty, the pin oak plays an important role in the habitat of Missouri waterfowl. Its tendency to grow in the moist soil along streams, often in solid stands, and to produce small, tasty acorns make it a favorite of waterfowl. These trees also support upland species such as songbirds, quail and even deer.

SHINGLE OAK
Quercus imbricaria
Fall Colors: Red-brown or yellow-brown.
Size: Up to 100 ft.
Description: A graceful tree with slender branches and a tall, rounded crown. Smooth gray bark, turning dark brown and becoming cracked with age.
Leaves: Elliptical with smooth edges, alternate on the stem. Dark green above, pale and hairy beneath. Wavy margins and a spiny tip. Acorns are small, somewhat flat and half-covered with a reddish-brown, scaly cap.
Where to find: Primarily in dry upland sites, also found throughout the bottomlands of the Missouri River. The name of this tree comes from the wood's tendency to split into shingles.

CHINKAPIN OAK
Quercus muehlenbergii
Fall Colors: Yellow, orangish-brown or brown.
Size: Up to 80 ft.
Description: Bark is ash gray and scaly.
Leaves: Looks like a chainsaw with deep, pointed teeth. Leaves are narrow and pointed, hairy underneath, 4–7 in. long. Acorns are about 1/2 in., rounded and only half-enclosed by a scaly cup.
Where to find: Glades and limestone-based soils.
Note: Acorns are sweet and were used by Native Americans to make acorn flour and meal.

WHITE OAK

Quercus alba

Fall Colors: Deep red or purple.

Size: Up to 100 ft.

Description: Has a broad, symmetrical crown and a straight trunk covered with light gray scaly bark.

Leaves: From 5 to 9 in. long. Each has 7–9 rounded lobes, which may be deep or shallow. Narrows at the stem. Its acorns are about 3/4 in. with pointed ends and warty scales that cover about 1/4 in. of the nut.

> **A NOTE ABOUT OAKS**
>
> During its five most active months, the average oak tree evaporates about 28,000 gallons of water. That's approximately 187 gallons each day.

Where to find: Likes deep, well-drained soils but will also grow in sandy places and on dry hillsides.

Note: The best known of all the oaks, this is an outstanding lumber tree and is the oak used for furniture, boats and barrels. A Missouri law dictates that all whiskey barrels produced in the state must be made from white oak.

Oak trees such as the prized **white oak** produce tremendous numbers of acorns. There is good reason for this—it has been estimated that it takes over 10,000 acorns to produce a single tree. The majority of the acorns are consumed by wildlife that share their habitat with these mighty trees. In fact, the acorns of the white oak provide one of the most important winter food sources for Missouri River valley wildlife.

BLACKJACK OAK

Quercus marilandica

Fall Colors: Yellow.

Size: Rarely more than 30–40 ft.

Description: Scraggly form. Bark is dark and very rough.

Leaves: Dark, shiny leaves are up to 7 in. long, leathery, generally much broader at the end than at the base. Under-surface is quite hairy. Lobes are ill-defined. Acorn measures about 1/2 in. Thick, scaly cup covers half of it.

Where to find: Rocky hillsides and dry, unfertile, acidic soils.

Note: Wood makes excellent charcoal. Also known as Scrub Oak.

The acorns of the **blackjack oak** are an important food source for squirrels, raccoons, quail, turkey and deer. The blackjack oaks and other members of the oak family played an important role in the development of Missouri forests due to their ability to resist and recover from fire damage. Oak trees, especially the blackjack variety, because of their extremely durable bark and ability to sprout, were often the first to reoccur after a major forest fire. Today's woodland fires, although potentially serious, rarely bother the members of the oak family and their fire retardant features have greatly determined the character of the state's forests.

BLACK WILLOW
Salix nigra
Fall Colors: Yellow-green.
Size: Up to 80 ft.
Description: Thick spreading branches form a broad irregular crown. Dark brown, almost black trunk, which is often twisted, curved or leaning. Dark brown, divided and shaggy.
Leaves: Narrow, fine-toothed, lance-like leaves with curved tips. Uniformly green, 3–6 in. long. Alternate down stem.
Where to find: Needs an abundant and continuous supply of moisture. Can be found along streams in swampy areas.
Note: Flowers are erect, downy catkins in spring before leaves appear. Sometimes are cut for "Pussy Willows."

Although there are many different types of willows in Missouri, the **black willow** is the largest. Willows collectively play an important role in stabilizing river and stream banks. These trees are fond of sunlight and are hardy opportunists, often the first to occupy vacant sand and gravel bars. Each of the various willows produce a light and flexible wood that is typically woven into baskets and wickerwork furniture. Young willows even just a few years old are often 6 feet tall and no bigger around than your pinkie.

SANDBAR WILLOW
Salix interior
Size: Up to 25 ft.
Description: Shrubby, often grow in thickets. Bark is thin, reddish-brown and scaly.
Leaves: From 2 to 7 in., very narrow, smooth on both sides, alternate with widely spaced teeth.
Where to find: On new sandbars and gravel banks along streams.
Note: Cuttings take root easily.

RIVER BIRCH
Betula nigra
Fall Colors: Dull yellow.
Size: Can grow to 70 ft. but more commonly less than 50 ft.
Description: Bark is red-brown. Has short hanging branches and thin twigs. Bark curls into thin sheets on young trees. Becomes shallow plates on older trunks.
Leaves: Oval, pointed with double-toothed margins. Generally 1–3 in. long. Turn dull yellow in autumn.
Where to find: Along stream banks and in wet woods where the soil is deep and moist.

BLACK HAW
Viburnum prunifolium
Fall Colors: Scarlet or burgundy red.
Size: Up to 20 ft. Often shrub-like.
Description: Smaller understory tree. Bark is gray and broken into thick, plate-like scales.
Leaves: Oblong, coarse to finely toothed. Opposite. Has clusters of tiny white flowers with 5 petals and blue-black berries.
Where to find: Along streams, rocky woodlands and old roads.
Note: This understory tree displays brilliant red or rich burgundy fall colors.

BUTTERNUT
Juglans cinerea
Fall Colors: Golden yellow.
Size: Up to 60 ft.
Description: Widespread round-topped crown. Stout limbs. Grayish bark that is smooth in young trees and divided by white ridges in older ones.
Leaves: Alternate, 15–20 in. long with 11–17 pointed, oblong, fine-toothed leaflets 2–3 in. long. Leaflets are finely haired underneath. The nuts are long and pointed, greenish-brown, sticky on the surface of the thick husk and good to eat.
Where to find: Likes rich, moist loamy soils. Often found along the edges of creeks, streams and rivers.
Note: Sometimes called White Walnut.

OHIO BUCKEYE
Aesculus glabra

Fall Colors: Pale yellow or tan.

Size: Up to 60 ft.

Description: Forms distinctive globular crown. Bark is ashen and often dark gray. In mature trees the bark is divided into scaly blocks.

Leaves: Five veined, toothed leaflets radiating from the end of the stem 7–9 in. wide. Flowers that bloom early in the spring are yellow, in spikes at twig ends. Fruits are large, shiny, dark brown and inedible. The white spot on the fruit is what gives the tree its name.

Where to find: Moist limestone areas, bottomlands and along stream banks.

Note: One of the first trees to display its leaves in the spring and the one of the first to lose them in the fall. Although **poisonous**, the seeds of this tree are supposed to bring good luck!

"Stinking buckeye" is another name by which that **Ohio buckeye** is commonly known. The name comes from the unpleasant odor that the bark, leaves and twigs produce when damaged or bruised. Although foul smelling, the leaves and roots contain a natural soap product that will generate a lather when rubbed in water.

SUMAC
Rhus glabra

Fall Colors: Red.

Size: Up to 20 ft. and shrub-like.

Description: Thick pithy branches. Bark appears gray and is relatively thin.

Leaves: From 16 to 25 in. long, narrow, lance-shaped, sharp-toothed, alternate, hairy and almost white underneath. Fruits form in compact, pyramid-shaped upright clusters up to 7 in. long. Greenish-yellow in color turning brilliant red in the fall.

Where to find: Old fields and edges of woodlands. Needs well-drained soil.

Note: Native Americans used to make flutes from the stalks.

SPICEBUSH
Lindera benzoin
Size: Up to 10 ft.
Description: Appears as a large shrub with slender twigs. Bark is thin and brown.
Leaves: Alternate, thick, pointed and much narrower at the base. Up to 12 in. long. Aromatic when crushed. This bush has male and female flowers on separate shrubs. Male flowers are showier and larger. Female flowers are in clusters on short stems along the branches. Blooms from March to May. Flowers turn into clusters of bright red berries that make this shrub very attractive in the fall.
Where to find: In wet woodlands and bottomlands.

Note: Member of the Laurel family, characterized by fragrant leaves and stems. Twigs gathered from the **spicebush** can be boiled to yield a pleasant tea with a distinctive purple color.

WAHOO
Euonymus atropurpureus
Fall Colors: Scarlet red.
Size: Up to 40 ft. Rarely exceeds 25 ft.
Description: Small tree with a small diameter trunk. Bark is thin, scaly and gray.
Leaves: Simple, fine toothed, opposite, 1–3 in. and narrow tip. Small purple flowers. Scarlet leaves in autumn. Red seeds.
Where to find: Moist soils along streams and woodland edges.
Note: Fashioned into arrows by early Native Americans. The seed capsules are often called Hearts a-Bustin.'

BLADDERNUT
Staphylea trifolia
Size: Up to 12 ft.
Description: Typically a shrub, sometimes grows to resemble a small tree. Smooth and shiny brown bark.
Leaves: Compound dark green leaves, 6–8 in., with 3 finely toothed leaflets. Opposite. White flowers are bell-shaped in drooping clusters. Blooms April to May. Fruits are lantern-shaped with brown, loose seeds inside.
Where to find: Edges of woods, in limestone soil, along streams and bluffs.
Note: The ripe fruit often grows in the direction of the prevailing winds.

HACKBERRY
Celtis—several species
Fall Colors: Green-yellow.
Size: Up to 40 ft.
Description: Bark is often gray. Can be completely smooth or covered with wart-like bumps and ridges.
Leaves: Uneven, veiny and oval. Sharp-toothed margins. Curved pointed tips. Fruit is tiny and deep purple when it is ripe.
Where to find: Moist soils in river and creek bottoms or along the base of ravines.
Note: The tough and flexible wood was used to make barrel hoops and is now used to produce shipping crates.

The **hackberry** fruit is edible, although its sugary pulp is often tainted with a variety of odd tastes. The fruit ripens in September and is an important winter food for many birds and animals.

SHADBUSH
Amelanchier arborer

Fall Colors: Yellow to apricot-orange to dull rusty red.

Size: Up to 30 ft.

Description: An understory tree with smooth, light-gray bark. Beautiful, early blooming spring tree.

Leaves: Hairy, oval, pointed leaves 2–4 in. Alternate. Flowers are white in drooping clusters with narrow petals, almost fringe-like, and bloom before leaves come out. A true sign of spring. Fruit is red to purple and sweet. Edible.

Where to find: Hillsides and open wooded areas. The fruit of this tree is often called Service Berry, Shad Blow, June Berry or May Cherry.

SASSAFRAS
Sassafras albidum

Fall Colors: Yellow, orange, purple or scarlet.

Size: Usually a shrub to 2 ft., but can be a tree growing to 60 ft.

Description: Typically grows in colonies.

Leaves: To 7 in., long, pointed, either unlobed or up to 3 lobes, not always the same size. Leaves narrow toward base. Turn golden in the fall. Crushed leaves have a spicy odor. Flowers are yellow-green and hang in clusters at ends of deep red branches, followed by dark red berries in clusters, which are relished by birds. The berries turn blue in autumn.

Where to find: In acid soils in dry woods, fields and along hedgerows.

Note: The aromatic oil found in the bark of its roots is one of the principal flavors in rootbeer. In early spring the young roots are used to make tea and, in Cajun country, the leaves are ground to produce the spice filo powder.

It is quite easy to make an aromatic tea from the **sassafras**. The most popular variety of the tea is produced from the roots. The root is steeped in water, which turns into a pleasant reddish tea. Keep making tea until the root loses its color.

PAWPAW

Asimina triloba

Fall Colors: Yellow to green.

Size: From 10 to 20 ft.

Description: An understory tree that often grows in thickets by sending up suckers from the roots.

Leaves: Large, up to 12 in., long, smooth and shaped like a wide oval. Green flowers begin blooming in March, but turn a maroon color with age. Have a strong smell like fermenting grapes. The fruit is like a small greenish-yellow banana and is good to eat when ripe, but hard to find as it is liked by many mammals.

Where to find: Rich soils and usually under taller trees in bottomland woods.

Note: Sometimes known as the Missouri Banana Tree.

Although the fruit of the **pawpaw** was a favorite of pioneers and is still consumed today, it has been known to nauseate some tasters. The pawpaw fruit is ripe in October and identified by its wrinkled black skin and soft flesh.

BOX ELDER

Acer negundo

Fall Colors: Brown.

Size: Up to 60 ft.

Description: Bark is pale gray or light brown, deeply divided and has scaly ridges. Divides near the ground into numerous branches. Forms a wide-spreading crown.

Leaves: Opposite. Looks somewhat like a maple. Has 3–9 coarse-toothed leaflets. The last leaflet is sometimes lobed. Winged seeds hang in tassel-like clusters.

Where to find: Along rivers and streams, but can adapt to a variety of areas.

Note: Sometimes called the Ash Leaf Maple. Very young trees, with their "leaves of 3" patterns, are often confused with Poison Ivy.

REDBUD
Cercis canadensis
Fall Colors: Yellow.
Size: Up to 25 ft.
Description: Brown bark is smooth on young trees, furrowed on older ones.
Leaves: Heart-shaped with smooth edges, 3–4 in. Alternate leaf arrangements. Lavender to red-purple flowers in March and April. Bean-like pods follow, becoming purple in late summer.
Where to find: Moist, wooded, usually shaded areas. Often grows in old fields, fencerows and woodland edges.
Note: Roots can be used to make a red dye.

FLOWERING DOGWOOD
Cornus florida
Fall Colors: Brilliant red.
Size: Up to 40 ft. but usually smaller and more shrub-like.
Description: Usually a shrub-like understory tree. Bark is red-brown.
Leaves: Opposite, 4 in. long by 2 in. wide. Tips pointed, bright green on top, pale green underneath. Flowers are 4-petaled and white and bloom from April to mid-May. Fruit is in red berry-like clusters and is sought after by many birds.
Where to find: Likes rich, moist soils. Often found along fencerows, field edges and open woodlands.
Note: Flower "petals" are actually a kind of leaf with the true flower in the center. Legend tells of this being the wood of the Holy Cross—with flowers showing the rusty nail imprints.

The **flowering dogwood** is the official state tree of Missouri. Though beautiful and popular, the origin of its common name isn't known. Need a toothpick? French natives in both Canada and Louisiana are known to use its twigs to clean and brighten their teeth.

RED OSIER DOGWOOD
Cornus stolonifera
Size: Up to 20 ft.
Description: Broad in shape. Bark turns crimson in winter.
Leaves: Opposite leaves are oval and veined. Flowers are creamy in domed heads, bloom in early summer. Has blue-black berries in August and September.
Where to find: Wet, moist areas along stream banks.

WHY DO TREES HAVE LEAVES?

The leaves of a tree act as the tree's lungs, skin and cooling system. Though leaves come in a broad range of sizes, they have one main function: to generate food for the tree. Leaves use the energy contained in sunlight to capture carbon from the air. This carbon, in turn, forms the basic building block that supports growth. Apart from that, trees "breathe" through their leaves and also lose water vapor.

FLOWERING PLANTS

Flowering plants are the highlight of any spring walk. As longer days, rising temperatures and increased rainfall signal the arrival of spring, many plants begin to bloom. Their colorful displays lure bees and other insects, which feed from the flowers and pollinate them, promoting the reproduction of many plant species.

To identify these flowering plants, you will find them listed first by color, going from lightest to darkest. Within each color section, flowers are further divided by the month they begin to bloom. If you are looking at a pink flower in April, for example, look under the color pink and then find April. The more you use the book, the more quickly you will be able to locate and identify new plants.

Be sure and visit your favorite places often, since the rebirth of the spring season delights visitors with new blooming arrivals every week. Also, weather patterns can affect when a plant blooms, so what you expect to see one week might actually bloom the next. The Missouri River valley contains so many flowers and variations that we don't have room to include all of them here. The following listings do, however, cover the most common varities you'll encounter.

Look for these tiny dots of color as you hike and enjoy the outdoors. Make your visit twice as nice by leaving the flowers to bloom and blanket the area with color. Leaving them to be enjoyed by others is the ethical and legal thing to do.

WHAT'S IN A NAME?

How do plants get their names? This is not an easy question to answer since most common names have been adapted from a wide variety of sources. Languages from all seven continents have influenced the English names we use, including Latin, Greek, German, French, Spanish and Native American just to name a few.

Additionally, various plant names have been assigned on the basis of the plant's shape, its resemblance to other natural creatures or human attributes, its use as a food, herb or medicine or the location where it typically grows.

Although the origin of common names is a serious study in itself, the plants listed in this guide are presented by their English common names, followed by their scientific names. The scientific naming provides an efficient scheme for pinpointing the true identity of any plant that you encounter. This two name, or binomial, system uses a Latin name that identifies each plant in terms of its genus name (the first name, always capitalized) which is followed by the species name (the second name, never capitalized). Also, these Latin names continue to change as new relationships are established between similar plants.

As you become familiar with the flora of the Missouri River valley try to figure out how the plants you observe got their names! Watch your friends turn in disbelief as you shout, "Look at that *Dicentra cucullaria!*"

A Sample Entry for Flowering Plants

COMMON NAME
Scientific Name
Family Name—Native or Non-Native.
Blooms: Indicates months when flowers are in bloom.
Habitat: Soil preferences and distribution.
Flowers: Features of flower including color and size.
Leaves and Stem: Includes size, shape and orientation.
Note: Other common names, interesting facts or trivia.

Using terms to identify plants

The lingo of flowering plants may seem a little technical and precise. Part of the difficulty of correctly identifying flowering plants in the Missouri River valley is that the science of taxonomy (how things are named) is constantly changing. Add to this that Missouri is home to a wide and varied collection of flowering plants—and the challenge of making a correct identification becomes even greater.

The list of terms on the next page will help you meet this challenge and increase your understanding of the flora in the region.

Alternate – Leaves located singly at intervals along stem.

Anther – Part of **stamen** that contains the pollen.

Bract – A small leaf-like structure that is near the flower.

Colony – A group of individual plants.

Compound Leaf – A leaf divided into 2 or more similar parts called **leaflets**.

Disk – The central tubular flowers in the flower **head** of the Daisy Family.

Evergreen – Stays green all winter long.

Female Flower – A flower with **pistils**, but no **stamens**.

Filament – Part of the **stamen** that supports the **anther**.

Habitat – The type of place in which the plant grows.

Head – A dense cluster of flowers.

Hood – Curved part of some flowers.

Leaflets – One of the leaf-like segments of a **compound leaf**.

Lobe – Part of a flower or leaf that bulges outward.

Male Flower – A flower with **stamens**, but no **pistils**.

Native – A plant that is natural to the area.

Opposite or paired – Leaves located directly across the stem from each other.

Ovary – Part of the **pistil** which contains the structures (ovules) that will become the seeds after fertilization.

Petal – Part of the flower that is usually brightly colored. Attracts insects.

Pistil – The female reproductive part of the flower consisting of a **stigma**, **style** and **ovary**.

Ray – The outer flowers in the flower **head** of the Daisy Family.

Rosette – Leaves arranged in a circle at the base of the plant.

Sepal – The most outer part of the flower, protects the flower when in bud. May be green or colored like the **petals**.

Sessile – Without a **stalk**.

Spike – A tall cluster of stalkless flowers.

Stalk – The main stem of a plant or flower cluster.

Stamen – The male reproductive part of a flower, consists of the **anther** and **filament**.

Stem – Main support structure of the plant.

Spur – Hollow sac-like or tubular structure on some flowers.

Stigma – A part of a flower that is the top parts of the **pistil** which receives the pollen.

Style – A part of a flower that is the long structure between the **ovary** and the **stigma**.

Tendril – A slender, coiled organ that attaches to other objects.

Whorl – Group of leaves arranged in circle around the stem.

White - January

HARBINGER OF SPRING
Also called Salt-and-Pepper.
Erigenia bulbosa
Carrot Family (Apiaceae). Native.
Blooms: January through April.
Habitat: Woodland plant often found along base of slopes and along streams. Occurs along river east from Boone County. Not in western section.
Flowers: A cluster of tiny flowers with 5 white petals and dark red stamens. Flowers barely protrude a few inches above the ground.
Leaves and Stem: Tiny plant, only a few inches above ground when flowering. Leaves divided and lacy like a carrot, usually come out after flowering. Stems are purple.

Note: Called Salt-and-Pepper due to the white petals and red anthers. You have to be a good observer to see this wildflower. Because of it small size and early flowering, it is easily overlooked. The first native wildflower along the Missouri River to bloom—the first true sign of spring in Missouri.

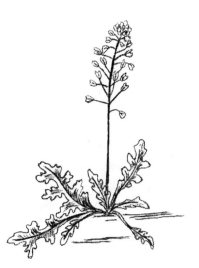

SHEPARD'S PURSE
Capsella bursa-pastoris
Mustard Family (Brassicaceae). Introduced, native of Europe.
Blooms: January through December.
Habitat: Open disturbed areas of fields, lawns and along roads.
Flowers: Tiny white flower with 4 petals. Seeds pods are flat and triangular or purse-shaped.
Leaves and Stem: Stem leaves are small, lance-shaped and clasp the stem. Leaves at the base of the plant (basal) are deeply lobed and divided, like a small dandelion leaf.
Note: Seeds can be used as a pepper substitute and young leaves in salads. The seeds and young leaves are frequently eaten by birds.

White - February

SPRING BEAUTY
Claytonia virginica
Purslane Family (Portulacaceae). Native.
Blooms: February through May.
Habitat: Open areas, woods, meadows and lawns. One of the most common spring wild-flowers.
Flowers: White flowers with 5 pink striped petals and 5 pink anthers. Two blunt sepals at base of flower (the only 5-petal, 2-sepal plant in Missouri).
Leaves and Stem: Only one pair of slender, grass-like leaves.
Note: Bulbs look like tiny new potatoes and are called "Fairy Spuds." Used by Native Americans as food and taste like chestnuts. Flowers open only in sunshine.

White - March

BLOODROOT
Also called Red Puccoon.
Sanguinaria canadensis
Poppy Family (Papaveraceae). Native.
Blooms: March through April.
Habitat: Rich bottomland woods near limestone rocks.
Flower: Single, bright white and showy flower, usually with 8 petals, surrounding many bright yellow stamens. Flowers are fragrant and short-lived, each flower lasts only one day.
Leaves and Stem: Single, large, pale-colored and heart-shaped leaf with 3–9 lobes. When flower first opens, leaf is wrapped around flower stem. Horizontal roots. Sap of plant is blood-red.
Note: Roots were used in medicine by native Americans and pioneers. Sap was used as body paint and dye by Native Americans. **Entire plant is poisonous.**

FALSE RUE ANEMONE
Isopyrum biternatum
Buttercup Family (Ranunculaceae). Native.
Blooms: March through May.
Habitat: Rich bottomland woods and along streams.
Flower: Showy white, 5 petal-like sepals—not true petals. Numerous yellow-green stamens. Flowers are always white.
Leaves and Stem: Each leaf divided into 3 or 9 leaflets, each with 3 lobes which are deeply divided and pointed. Roots thread-like.
Note: Very similar to Rue Anemone, only different habitat and flower colors. Forms beautiful carpet of flowers along streams in early spring.

TOOTHWORT
Cardamine concatenata
Mustard Family (Brassicaceae). One of the few showy members of this family. Native.
Blooms: March through May.
Habitat: Rich or rocky woodlands.
Flowers: White flowers tinged with pink or lavender. The 4 petals fuse into tube at base, but ends of petals form a cross.
Leaves and Stem: Umbrella-like whorl of 3 stem leaves, each leaf is divided into long, narrow, toothed lobes. Horizontal root looks like animal teeth.
Note: Roots have horseradish-like flavor.

White – Late March

DUTCHMAN'S BREECHES
Dicentra cucullaria
Bleeding Heart Family (Fumariaceae). Native.
Blooms: Late March through May.
Habitat: Rich and moist rocky woods, often in ravines
Flower: White or very light pink flowers tipped with yellow. The 3–12 nodding flowers are v-shaped and look like inflated pants hung upside down in a row.
Leaves and Stem: Grayish-green, fern-like leaves all come from base of plant.
Note: Contain an alkaloid that is **Poisonous**. Resembles its cousin, the Bleeding Heart.

MAY APPLE
Also called Mandrake
Podophyllum peltatum
Barberry Family
(Berberidaceae). Native.
Blooms: Late March through
May, fruit usually ripens in
July and August.
Habitat: Open woods. Always
occurs in colonies.
Flower: Single, large, white
flower with 6–9 waxy petals
and yellow stamens. Flower
nodding on flower stalk, below
leaves.

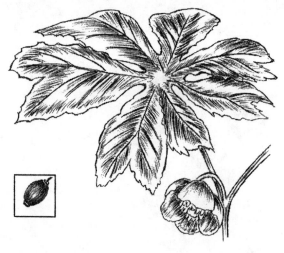

Leaves and Stem: Large umbrella-shaped leaves, each leaf with 5–9 lobes. One
leaf on non-flowering plants and two leaves on flowering plants. Horizontal roots.
Note: Both leaves and roots are **poisonous** and may cause rash when handling.
The fruit may be eaten when it is ripe and pale yellow. Roots were used in some
early medicines.

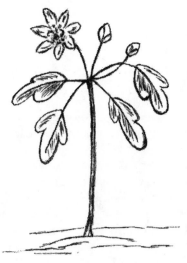

RUE ANEMONE
Anemonella thalictroides
Buttercup Family (Ranunculaceae). Native.
Blooms: Late March through June.
Habitat: Upper slopes of dry rocky woods.
Flower: Showy white or pink 5–10 petal-like
sepals—not true petals. Numerous yellow-
green stamens.
Leaves and Stem: Each leaf divided into 3
leaflets each, with 3 rounded shallow lobes.
Roots form a cluster of tubers.
Note: Very similar to False Rue Anemone,
but for different habitat and leaves. An ex-
ample of 2 plants that followed a similar evo-
lutionary path.

WHITE TROUT LILY
Also called White Dogtooth Violet.
Erythronium albidum
Lily Family (Liliaceae). Native.
Blooms: Late March and April.
Habitat: Moist bottomland woods along streams. Often grow in large colonies.
Flowers: Single, showy, nodding white flowers with large yellow stamens. Three white petals, and 3 petal-like sepals. The petals and sepals curl back as they open.
Leaves and Stem: On flowering plants, 2 oval shaped, pointed leaves coming from base of plant. Single leaves on sterile, non-flowering plants. Leaves mottled with brown and silver suggesting the coloration of a trout.
Note: Also called White Dog-Tooth Violet or Fawn Lily. The first Lily in Missouri to bloom in the spring.

WHITE — APRIL

PHILADELPHIA FLEABANE
Erigeron philadelphicus
Daisy Family (Asteraceae). Native.
Blooms: From April to June.
Habitat: Open dry woods.
Flowers: Small daisy-like flower heads with numerous white to pink ray flowers surrounding a large yellow central disk.
Leaves and Stem: Leaves at base of plant are egg-shaped with blunt tips. Leaves on stem are smaller, spear-shaped, sharp-pointed and clasp the stem.
Note: Medieval Europeans believed that related plants kept fleas away. Also was used as a medicinal plant. **May cause skin rash.**

PUSSY'S TOES
Antennaria plantaginifolia
Daisy Family (Asteraceae). Native.
Blooms: April through June.
Habitat: Dry, rocky and open woods. Usually grow in colonies.
Flowers: Round, fuzzy and cotton-ball-like, white flower heads at end of stalk.
Leaves and Stem: Leaves at base of plant are large and spoon-shaped with 3–5 veins. Leaves on stem are narrow and without stalks. A short, woolly plant.
Note: Leaves at base of plant stay green all winter and provide an important winter food for deer and other animals. Plant was used medicinally. A similar plant (*Antennaria neglecta*) has only one main vein on its basal leaf.

STAR-OF-BETHLEHEM
Ornithogalum umbellatum
Lilly Family (Liliaceae).
Introduced, native of Europe.
Blooms: April through June.
Habitat: Open fields, grassy places and along shaded streams.
Flowers: White upright flowers with 3 petals and 3 petal-like sepals. Petals and sepals have green line on back.
Leaves and Stem: Thick clump of narrow, grass-like, dark green leaves with white midribs. Short plant produces bulbs at a rapid rate.
Note: This escaped garden plant is **poisonous** and may push native plants out of an area.

WATERCRESS
Rorippa nasturtium-aquaticum
(formerly *Nasturtium officinale*)
Mustard Family (Brassicaceae).
Introduced, native of Europe.
Blooms: April through October.
Habitat: In and around springs and spring-fed streams. Grow in colonies.
Flowers: Many tiny 4-petaled white flowers in groups at end of stems.
Leaves and Stem: Bright green leaves divided into 3 or more rounded leaflets. Stems float on water.
Note: Peppery flavored leaves are used in salads.

WILD STRAWBERRY
Fragaria virginiana
Rose Family (Rosaceae). Native.
Blooms: April through May.
Habitat: Open areas in old fields, prairies and edges of woods.
Flowers: Several flowers on each plant, each with 5 white round petals and many stamens.
Leaves and Stem: Leaves divided into 3 leaflets. Each leaflet is egg-shaped and toothed. Stem is hairy. Plant is spread by "runners" coming out of base of plant.
Note: The ripe berries are smaller and sweeter than those of the cultivated type.

White – May

AMERICAN FEVERFEW
Also called Wild Quinine
Parthenium integrifolium
Daisy Family (Asteraceae). Native.
Blooms: May through September.
Habitat: Prairies, glades and dry open woods. Absent from the northwest counties.
Flowers: Flat-topped cluster of small, 1/4 in.-wide, numerous, white flower heads each with 5 tiny ray flowers.
Leaves and Stem: Leaves at base (basal) are large (up to 8 in.), egg-shaped, toothed, rough-surfaced and long stalked.
Note: Was used medicinally to treat fevers and may actually stimulate the immune system. **May cause skin rash**.

FLOWERING SPURGE
Euphorbia corollata
Spurge Family (Euphorbiaceae). Native.
Blooms: May through October.
Habitat: Prairies, glades, fields, open woods and along roads.
Flowers: Flat, open and branched cluster of small, 1/4 in.-wide, white flowers. The 5 white "petals" are really bracts that surround the tiny flowers in the cup.
Leaves and Stem: A whorl of leaves just below the flower cluster. Rest of stalkless, linear leaves are alternate. Milky juice in stem. Plant is 1–3 ft. tall.
Note: Causes rashes and is a strong laxative in humans. Poisonous to livestock. Plant is often eaten by wild turkey and deer. Used medicinally by native Americans.

GOAT'S BEARD
Aruncus dioicus
Rose Family (Rosaceae). Native.
Blooms: May through July.
Habitat: Moist, rich woods.
Flowers: Tiny, creamy white flowers with 5 petals on long branching plumes.
Leaves and Stem: Most of the leaves from base of plant and are divided 2 to 3 times into toothed leaflets. A tall plant.
Note: The male and female flowers are on separate plants. Used medicinally by Native Americans.

OX-EYE DAISY
Leucanthemum vulgare
(formerly *Chrysanthemum leucanthemum*)
Daisy Family (Asteraceae).
Introduced, native of Europe.
Blooms: May through August.
Habitat: Prairies, fields and roadsides.
Flowers: One large, 2 in.-wide, flower head on a long stalk. Flower head with 15–30 white rays surrounding a yellow disk with a depressed center.
Leaves and Stem: Narrow, lobed or toothed leaves. Plant is typically 1–3 ft. tall.
Note: One of the most beautiful and familiar daisy-like flowers. Young leaves can be used in salads.

POISON HEMLOCK
Conium maculatum
Carrot Family (Apiaceae).
Introduced, native of Europe.
Blooms: May through August.
Habitat: Fields, disturbed areas and along roads.
Flowers: Flat-topped cluster of tiny white flowers.
Leaves and Stem: Dark green, finely divided and fern-like leaves. Stems are smooth and spotted with purple. Plant has many branches and gives off an unpleasant smell when cut.
Note: All parts of this plant are poisonous. This is the plant that killed Socrates. One of the most poisonous plants in Missouri.

QUEEN ANNE'S LACE
Also called Wild Carrot.
Daucus carota
Carrot Family (Apiaceae). Native of Europe and Asia.
Blooms: May through October.
Habitat: Fields, along roads and other open areas.
Flowers: Tiny, white or tinged with pink, flowers in lacy, flat-topped clusters. Center flower of cluster is purple. After flowering the cluster curls inward, forming a "bird's nest."
Leaves and Stem: Leaves are very finely divided. Has a large taproot.
Note: It is an ancestor of the garden carrot. It can take-over large areas and is considered a weed by farmers.

SMOOTH BEARD–TONGUE
Penstemon digitalis
Figwort Family (Scrophulariaceae). Native.
Blooms: May and June
Habitat: Fields, prairies and borders of woods. Often grow in colonies.
Flowers: White, tubular flowers are in loose spike-like cluster at end of stem. Each flower has 2 upper lobes and three lower lobes and one of the stamens in the center has tufts of hairs.
Leaves and Stem: Lance-shaped, opposite (paired) leaves that are toothed and stalkless. Stem smooth and 2–4 feet tall.
Note: Gets name from the hairy stamen, which looks like a tongue. Used to attract insects.

SOLOMON'S SEAL
Polygonatum biflorum
Lilly Family (Liliaceae). Native.
Blooms: May and June
Habitat: Rich bottomland woods.
Flowers: Greenish-white, tubular flowers hanging bell-like in clusters beneath arching stem. Has dark blue berries by late summer.
Leaves and Stem: Oval leaves are alternate and clasping on arching stem and has parallel leaf veins.
Note: When the stem of plant is broken from the root it leaves a scar which resembles the official seal of King Solomon. Native Americans and settlers used the starchy root in foods and medicines.

WHITE CLOVER
Trifolium repens
Pea Family (Fabaceae).
Non-native, native of Europe and Asia.
Blooms: May through October.
Habitat: Lawns, fields, along roads and other open areas. One of the world's most widespread plants.
Flowers: White to light pink pea-like flowers in a rounded flower head on a long flower stalk.
Leaves and Stem: Leaves arising on separate stalks from a creeping stem. Leaf made of 3 slightly toothed leaflets with light green "v" markings.
Note: Good for use in soil improvement, erosion control and wildlife food. Clover honey comes from this species and Red Clover.

WHITE WILD INDIGO
Baptisia alba (formerly *Baptisia leucantha*)
Pea Family (Fabaceae). Native.
Blooms: May through July.
Habitat: Prairies, glades, fields, along streams, levees and roads.
Flowers: White, 1 in.-long, pea-shaped flowers on long upright stalks.
Leaves and Stem: Leaves divided into three smooth-edged (entire) leaflets. Plant without hairs. From 2 to 5 ft. tall.
Note: The leaves produce a poor kind of indigo dye when old and dried. Was used medicinally. **May be poisonous.**

WHITE ANEMONE
Also called Meadow Anemone.
Anemone canadensis
Buttercup Family (Ranunculaceae). Native.
Blooms: May through July.
Habitat: Low moist ground of Missouri or Mississippi River flood plains. Grow in large colonies.
Flowers: Showy, single, white flower on long stem. Five white petal-like sepals and many yellow stamens.
Leaves and Stem: Leaves are 3-divided, stalkless (sessile) and surround the stem. Leaves at base (basal) are 3-divided and have stalks. Commonly 1–3 ft. tall.
Note: One of the few plants that occurs mainly along the Missouri and Mississippi rivers of the state. Covers the levees with beautiful white flowers.

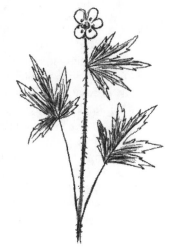

WHITE SWEET CLOVER
Melilotus albus
Pea Family (Fabaceae).
Introduced, native of Asia.
Blooms: May through October.
Habitat: Open ground in fields and along roads.
Flowers: Tiny, white, pea-shaped flowers on long and slender spikes. Flowers have strong perfume and its fragrance is produced over a long period of time.
Leaves and Stem: Leaves are divided into 3 leaflets. Each leaflet is narrow, rounded at top and finely toothed.
Note: Along with the Yellow Sweet Clover, this plant is valued by bees for honey production and planted as a pasture crop. Its presence in an area suggests that the native flora has been disturbed. Arrived in Missouri in about 1887.

YARROW
Also called Common Milfoil or Nosebleed.
Achillea millefolium
Daisy Family (Asteraceae).
Introduced, native of Europe and Asia.
Blooms: May through November.
Habitat: Prairies, fields and roadsides.
Flowers: Tiny, white or rarely pink, 5 ray flower heads with pale yellow central disk in a flat, dense cluster.
Leaves and Stem: Soft, finely dissected, fern-like leaves with a pungent odor. Plant typically grows to be 1–2 ft. tall.
Note: Plant is weedy and spread by its roots which makes it difficult to eradicate. Used as a medicinal plant—over 100 biological active compounds have been identified in this plant. Dried plants used in flower arrangements. **May cause skin irritation and may be toxic.**

WILD GARLIC

Also called Wild Onion.

Allium canadenses

Lily Family (Liliaceae). Native.

Blooms: May through July.

Habitat: Moist open bottomland woods, prairies, fields and along roads.

Flowers: Erect cluster of small bulbs with a few white or pink flowers.

Leaves and Stem: Very narrow and grass-like. Flat leaves with strong onion smell.

Note: Can be used as a substitute for onions.

WHITE – LATE MAY

WATER HEMLOCK

Also called Spotted Cowbane.

Cicuta maculata

Carrot Family (Apiaceae). Native.

Blooms: Late May through September.

Habitat: Wet bottomland areas around ponds, streams and ditches.

Flowers: A loose flat-topped cluster of tiny, white flowers.

Leaves and Stem: The alternate leaves are divided once or twice into toothed, lance-shaped leaflets with a red tinge. The stem is smooth and streaked with purple. The stem also bears many leafy branches.

Note: All parts of this plant are deadly poisonous. This plant is easily confused with the Wild Carrot and the Wild Parsnip.

JIMSONWEED

Datura stramonium

Nightshade Family (Solanaceae).

Native of tropical America.

Blooms: Late May through October.

Habitat: Fields, disturbed areas and along roads.

Flowers: Large, 3–5 in. long, trumpet-shape, white or pale violet flowers. Flowers open at sunset, close at sunrise and give off a strong perfume. Fruit is contained in a 2 in., spiny pod.

Leaves and Stem: Alternate, egg-shaped, coarsely toothed and pointed leaves. Often with purple stems. Plant has an unpleasant smell.

Note: Plant contains atropine that is used to dilate eye pupils. **This plant is very toxic, even deadly**.

POKEWEED

Also called Poke.
Phytolacca americana
Pokeweed Family (Phytolaccaceae).
Native.
Blooms: Late May through October
Habitat: Disturbed areas, fields and along roads.
Flowers: Slender cluster of greenish-white small flowers with 5 petal-like sepals. Drooping cluster of dark purple berries with red stalks.
Leaves and Stem: Alternate, large, smooth-edged and lance-shaped leaves. Stout, juicy, branching and reddish stem.
Note: The red juice of the berries has been used as a dye. A collection of the young leaves—a Poke Salad—is eaten by some people in the spring. **The mature plant is poisonous.**

White – June

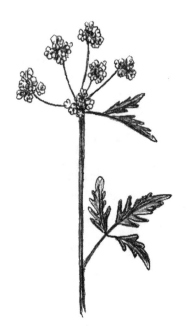

HEDGE PARSLEY

Torilis nodosa
Carrot Family (Apiaceae).
Introduced, native of Europe and Asia.
Blooms: June through August.
Habitat: Dry, open places and disturbed areas such as fields and roadsides.
Flowers: Tiny, white flowers in small, flat clusters on long stems well above the leaves.
Leaves and Stem: Leaves are parsley-like and divided once or twice into leaflets. Stem is hairy and branched.
Note: Seeds have hooks that cling to clothes and fur. Plant introduced relatively recently to Missouri in 1909.

White - Late July

WHITE SNAKEROOT
Eupatorium rugosum
Daisy Family (Asteraceae). Native.
Blooms: Late July through October.
Habitat: Woods and thickets.
Flowers: Tiny, bright white flowers heads in broad, branching cluster.
Leaves and Stem: Long-pointed, toothed, opposite and heart-shaped leaves on slender stalks.
Note: This is a very **poisonous** plant to people and livestock. When cows eat this plant, the poison is transferred to the milk. Many settlers in the Midwest, including Abraham Lincoln's mother, reportedly died from "milk sickness" caused by drinking the poisoned milk.

White - August

WHITE HEATHER ASTER
Aster pilosus
Daisy Family (Asteraceae). Native.
Blooms: August through November.
Habitat: Dry open places in fields, prairies and along roads.
Flowers: Numerous, small, 1/2 in.-wide, daisy-like flower-head with white rays and yellow center disk.
Leaves and Stem: Stiff, narrow and alternate leaves without stalks.
Note: The latest blooming White Aster. Deer love to browse Asters.

Yellow - March

ORANGE PUCCOON
Also called Hoary Puccoon.
Lithospermun canescens
Borage Family (Boraginaceae). Native.
Blooms: March through June.
Habitat: Rocky open woods, glades, prairies and bluffs.
Flowers: Brilliant yellow-orange to orange tubular flowers with 5 flaring lobes. Flowers in curved cluster at end of stem.
Leaves and Stem: Leaves narrow and alternate. Covered with fine white hairs.
Note: Puccoon is a Native American word for any plant that produces red dye. Early settlers also used the roots to dye their clothes.

YELLOW VIOLET
Viola pubescens (formerly *Viola pensylvanica*)
Violet Family (Violaceae). Native.
Blooms: March through May.
Habitat: Rich woodlands on slopes and along streams.
Flowers: Bright yellow, violet-like flowers with purple veins near base of lower petals.
Leaves and Stem: Leaves from both base and stem are heart-shaped and finely scalloped. Leaves and flowers on same stalk.
Note: One of the first yellow spring wildflowers to bloom in this area.

YELLOW - APRIL

BELLWORT
Uvularia grandiflora
Lily Family (Liliaceae). Native.
Blooms: April through May.
Habitat: Rich woods on slopes and along streams.
Flowers: Bright yellow, long nodding flowers with 3 petals and 3 petal-like sepals.
Leaves and Stem: Oval leaves are bright green above and downy white underneath with base completely surrounding the stem. Stems are forked with 1 flower per fork. The leaves drop when the plant flowers.
Note: This beautiful Lily was used by Native Americans to treat pain. Seedpod resembles a bell.

COMMON CINQUEFOIL
Also called Five Finger.
Potentilla simplex
Rose Family (Rosaceae). Native.
Blooms: April through June.
Habitat: Fields, prairies and open woods.
Flowers: Yellow with 5 round petals.
Leaves and Stem: Divided into 5 sharply toothed leaflets all arising from one point. A low, creeping and hairy plant.
Note: Cinquefoil is French for "5-leaves". A favorite food for deer. New leaves make a good tea that is high in calcium.

PALE CORDYALIS
Also called Yellow Fumewort or Yellow Harlequin.
Corydalis flavula
Bleeding Heart Family (Fumariaceae). Native.
Blooms: April and May.
Habitat: Rich, moist bottomland woods along streams or below bluffs. Often grow in colonies.
Flowers: Small, pale yellow, drooping flowers with small spurs. Flowers are attached to stem near center.
Leaves and Stem: Finely lobed fern-like, blue-green leaves. Short and delicate plant.
Note: In the same family as Dutchman's Breeches. Has one of the more interesting flower shapes of the early spring wildflowers, but is easy to overlook. **Plant is toxic.** Native Americans used it medicinally.

SWAMP BUTTERCUP
Ranunculus hispidus
Buttercup Family (Ranunculaceae). Native.
Blooms: April through June.
Habitat: Rich woodlands on slopes along streams.
Flowers: Bright yellow showy flowers that have 5 shiny "buttered" petals with rounded tips. Flowers have numerous stamens and pistils.
Leaves and Stem: Deep green leaves divided into 3 deeply lobed parts with large teeth. Stems are hollow and often creeping or lying on ground.
Note: There are 18 species of buttercups that occur throughout the Missouri River valley, with this being the most common one. Pollinated by flies and bees. **All buttercups are acrid and can cause skin rashes.**

WOOD BETONY
Also called Common Lousewort.
Pedicularis canadensis
Figwort Family (Scrophulariaceae). Native.
Blooms: April and May.
Habitat: In acidic soil of dry open woods and along streams. Often grow in dense colonies.
Flowers: Light greenish-yellow, hooded flowers with a long curved upper lip and a 3-lobed lower lip. Flowers in dense whorls at top of flower stalk.
Leaves and Stem: Leaves are lance-shaped, deeply lobed and fern-like. In spring, leaves are often bright red.
Note: Plants are semi-parasitic, getting some of their food from the roots of other plants. A medicinal plant used by Native Americans.

YELLOW STAR GRASS
Hypoxis hirsuta
Lilly Family (Liliaceae). Native.
Blooms: April and May.
Habitat: Glades, prairies and dry open woods.
Flowers: Bright yellow flowers with 3 petals and 3 petal-like sepals.
Leaves and Stem: Grass-like leaves arise from base of plant. Plant is hairy.
Note: Seeds are a favorite of quail. Not really a grass—the grass-like leaves give it its name.

YELLOW ROCKET

Also called Common Winter Cress.

Barbarea vulgaris

Mustard Family (Brassicaceae). Introduced, native of Europe.

Blooms: April through June.

Habitat: Wet open areas near streams, fields and roadsides.

Flowers: Bright yellow with 4 petals in the shape of a cross.

Leaves and Stem: Two types of leaves, lower leaves divided into 5 lobes with the terminal lobe large and rounded. Upper stem leaves deeply lobed and clasping stem. Leafy plant with numerous branches.

Note: Leaves remain green all winter. Often forms showy yellow patches in open fields. Plant used by Native Americans for food and medicine. **Do not eat, may cause kidney problems.**

YELLOW — MAY

BLACK-EYED SUSAN

Rudbeckia hirta

Daisy Family (Asteraceae). Native.

Blooms: May through October.

Habitat: Prairies, old fields and along roads.

Flowers: Single, 3 in.-wide flower head with 10–20 dark yellow rays around a dark brown center disk.

Leaves and Stem: Alternate, hairy, thick, lance-shaped leaves without stalks. Stem is very hairy.

Notes: Native Americans used this plant for many medicinal uses. A favorite plant for deer.

COMMON GROUND CHERRY
Physalis longifolia
Nightshade Family (Solanaceae). Native.
Blooms: May through September.
Habitat: Moist areas in bottomland woods, along streams and borders of ponds and sloughs.
Flowers: Bell-shaped yellow to greenish-yellow flowers with brown central markings. Flowers hang singly from the base of the leaves. Fruit is enclosed in a 5-sided paper-like husk and looks like a Chinese lantern.
Leaves and Stem: Alternate, long stalked, egg-shaped leaves with un-symmetrical margins. This is a branching plant.
Note: The fruit inside the lantern tell you this plant is a relative of the tomato.

LANCE-LEAVED LOOSESTRIFE
Lysimachia lanceolata
Primrose Family (Primulaceae). Native.
Blooms: May through August.
Habitat: Prairies, woods and thickets. Found in central and eastern counties only.
Flowers: The flowers have 5-pointed yellow lobes that all come from the base of upper leaves.
Leaves and Stem: Leaves are opposite (paired) and lance-shaped, with narrow bases.
Notes: Named after King Lysimachos (means "ending strife") of ancient Thrace.

WILD PARSNIP
Pastinaca sativa
Carrot Family (Apiaceae). Introduced, native of Europe and Asia.
Blooms: May though October.
Habitat: Fields and roadsides.
Flowers: A flat-topped cluster of very small, pale yellow flowers.
Leaves and Stem: Alternate leaves are divided into 5–15 opposite (pinnate) sharply toothed leaflets. Stout, deeply-grooved stem.
Note: This is the garden parsnip that escaped. Similar to the poisonous Water Hemlock (*Cicuta maculata*), so it is best to grow your own and not to use the wild form.

YELLOW GOAT'S BEARD
Tragopogon dubius
Daisy Family (Asteraceae). Introduced, native of Europe.
Blooms: May through August.
Habitat: Open areas in fields, pastures and along roads.
Flowers: Single, yellow flower head with long slender green bracts that extend past the rays. Flowers form large, 3 in.-wide, dandelion-like seed heads.
Leaves and Stem: Grass-like leaves. Stem swollen just below flower head.
Note: Flowers open in morning and close by noon.

Yellow – Late May

EASTERN PRICKLY PEAR CACTUS

Opuntia humifusa (formerley *Opuntia compressa*)

Cactus Family (Cactaceae). Native.

Blooms: Late May through July.

Habitat: Rocky or sandy places in glades, prairies and fields.

Flowers: Large, 2–3 in.-wide, yellow flowers with many colored petals and sepals, often with reddish center. Yields a red, fleshy and pear-shaped, edible fruit.

Leaves and Stem: The leaf-like jointed green pads with gray or brown spines and bristles—these are actually the stems.

Note: The only native cactus along the Missouri River. **Bristles are hard to remove from the skin.**

ORANGE DAY LILY

Hemerocallis fulva

Lily Family (Liliaceae). Introduced, native of Europe and Asia.

Blooms: Late May through August.

Habitat: Escaped from gardens to fields, abandoned homes and along roadsides. Grow in thick colonies.

Flowers: Large, 3 in.-wide, funnel-shaped, 6-lobed, orange flower with yellow center and without spots. Flowers on a leafless stalk. Each flower lasts for only one day.

Leaves and Stem: Long, narrow, grass-like leaves coming from the base of the plant.

Note: This plant is sterile and does not produce seeds, it spreads by its roots. All parts of the plant have been used as food. **Be careful, the roots and young shoots may contain toxic chemicals.**

MULLEIN
Also called Flannel Plant.
Verbascum thapsus
Figwort Family (Scrophulariaceae). Introduced, native of Europe.
Blooms: Late May through September.
Habitat: Dry fields, disturbed areas and along roads.
Flowers: Dense, club-like, tall spike of 1-in.-wide yellow flowers.
Leaves and Stem: Large, soft, very hairy and flannel-like leaves, largest at base of plant.
Notes: A wild sunflower whose leaves and flower stalk were used medicinally for colds. The leaves and seeds contain toxins that can poison fish. Livestock will not eat this plant.

SPOTTED TOUCH-ME-NOT
Also called Jewel Weed.
Impatiens capensis
Touch-me-not Family (Balsaminaceae). Native.
Blooms: Late May through October.
Habitat: Moist bottomland woods and open areas. Occur in large colonies.
Flowers: The reddish-orange flower has brown spots on the petals and a curved spur or sack in back. Hang jewel-like from long flower stalk. Ripe seedpods explode when touched and throw out seeds.
Leaves and Stem: Egg-shaped, coarsely toothed and alternate, bluish green leaves. Juicy stems.

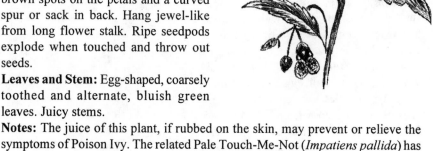

Notes: The juice of this plant, if rubbed on the skin, may prevent or relieve the symptoms of Poison Ivy. The related Pale Touch-Me-Not (*Impatiens pallida*) has a pale yellow flower and may be found along with this plant.

Yellow - June

BROWN-EYED SUSAN
Rudbeckia triloba
Daisy Family (Asteraceae). Native.
Blooms: June though November.
Habitat: Bottomland woods and along streams.
Flowers: Numerous, 1 in.-wide, daisy-like flower heads with 8–12 wide, yellow rays around a dark brown center disk.
Leaves and Stem: Alternate leaves are thin and hairy, may have course teeth. Some of the lower leaves are 3-lobed while the rest of the leaves are lance-shaped. Plant is branched with hairy stems.
Note: Can be told from the Black-Eyed Susan by the smaller flowers with fewer and wider rays and the lower 3-lobbed leaves (these are usually dried up by flowering time).

PARTRIDGE PEA
Chamaecrista fasciculata (formerly *Cassia fasciculata*)
Pea Family (Fabaceae). Native.
Blooms: June through October.
Habitat: Open places in prairies, fields and along roads.
Flowers: Large, showy, single, pea-shaped, yellow flower with wide petals and a brownish center, at base of the leaves. Has pea-like seedpod.
Leaves and Stem: Alternate, leaves divided into 6–15 small, egg-shaped leaflets tipped with bristles. Leaflets sometimes are sensitive or fold-up when touched.
Note: Seeds are a favorite food of wild turkey, quail and other game birds. When the seedpod ripens, it scatters the seeds a good distance away from the plant.

SPOTTED ST. JOHN'S-WORT

Hypericum punctatum
St. John's-Wort Family (Clusiaceae). Native.
Blooms: June through September.
Habitat: Prairies, old fields, open woods and roadsides.
Flowers: Crowed cluster of small flowers. Each flower has 5 yellow petals with black dots and many stamens.
Leaves and Stem: Opposite (paired), smooth-edged lance-shaped leaves, without stalks. Leaves and stem covered with black dots.
Note: Six other species of St. John's-Worts can be found along the Missouri River.

YELLOW – LATE JUNE

VELVET LEAF

Also called Butter-Print or Indian Mallow.
Abutilon theophrasti
Mallow Family (Malvaceae). Introduced, native of India.
Blooms: Late June through October
Habitat: Open places of fields, along roads and other disturbed areas. Very fast growing.
Flowers: Yellow, 1 in.-wide, 5-petaled flower coming from the base of the leaves. The top of the capsule-like fruit has a circular "beak" sticking out.
Leaves and Stem: Alternate, very large, heart-shaped and shallowly toothed leaves with pointed tip and velvet-like surface.
Note: The beak of the fruit was used to decorate the edge of pie crusts and reminded farmers of the print block used to stamp rolls of butter. Plant is used medicinally in Asia.

YELLOW - JULY

COMMON SUNFLOWER
Helianthus annuus
Daisy Family (Asteraceae). Native.
Blooms: July through November.
Habitat: Open areas in fields, prairies, disturbed areas and along roads.
Flowers: Many large, 3–5 in.-wide, flower heads with yellow rays with dark center disks.
Leaves and Stem: Large, alternate, lance-shaped (almost heart-shaped), toothed, rough leaves with long stalks.
Note: This is the wild ancestor of the cultivated sunflower (*Helianthus annuua var. macrocarpus*) which has larger flower heads. First cultivated by Native Americans who used the high protein and oily seeds for flour and oil. This is one of the more important foods that North America Native Americans introduced to the world.

COMPASS PLANT
Also called Rosinweed.
Silphium laciniatum
Daisy Family (Asteraceae). Native.
Blooms: July through September.
Habitat: Rocky places in prairies and glades.
Flowers: Large, 2 1/2 in.-wide, sunflower-like, yellow flower heads on upper stem.
Leaves and Stem: Huge, 1 1/2 ft.-wide, deeply lobed and stiff leaves.
Note: When the plant grows in full sunlight, it turns the edges of the leaves at the base of the plant so they point north and south. The upper stem secretes a gummy sap that was used by Native Americans as chewing gum.

CUP PLANT
Also called Cup Rosinweed or Carpenter's Weed.
Silphium perfoliatum
Daisy Family (Asteraceae). Native.
Blooms: July through September.
Habitat: Moist bottomland along streams and ponds, fields and roadsides.
Flowers: Large, 2–3 in.-wide, yellow sunflower-like flower heads with many rays and a dark yellow center disk.
Leaves and Stem: Opposite, egg-shaped leaves. The upper leaves unite at the base to form a cup.
Note: The leaf cup holds water following rain. Used medicinally by Native Americans and settlers to stop bleeding.

WILD SENNA
Senna marilandica
(formerly *Cassia marilandica*)
Pea Family (Fabaceae). Native.
Blooms: July through August.
Habitat: Moist bottomland woods, fields and roadsides.
Flowers: Cluster of bright yellow pea-shaped flowers with narrow petals and brownish center at base of the leaves. Flowers are smaller than those of the Partridge Pea. Long, jointed seedpods.
Leaves and Stem: The alternate leaves are divided into 5–10 pairs of egg-shaped leaflets. Rounded gland at base of leafstalk.
Note: Leaves are used medicinally as a strong laxative.

WILD LETTUCE
Lactuca canadensis
Daisy Family (Asteraceae). Native.
Blooms: July through September
Habitat: Woodlands, fields, bottomlands and along roads.
Flowers: Small, pale-yellow, dandelion-like flower heads.
Leaves and Stem: Leaves vary from deeply lobed to arrow-shaped and clasping. A tall branched plant with smooth stem.
Note: Plant has a bitter-tasting substance that was used medicinally as a nerve tonic. **Plant may be poisonous**.

Yellow - August

JERUSALEM ARTICHOKE
Helianthus tuberosus
Daisy Family (Asteraceae). Native.
Blooms: August through October.
Habitat: Moist open bottomlands, prairies and along roads.
Flowers: Large (3 in.-wide), sunflower-like flower head with yellow rays and darker yellow center disk. Bracts just below flower heads are long and pointed.
Leaves and Stem: Egg-shaped, toothed, rough, hairy. Lower leaves are opposite (paired) and upper leaves are alternate. Stem is rough and hairy.
Note: The plant is cultivated for its edible, potato-like root. The flower omits a chocolate scent.

SHOWY GOLDENROD
Solidago speciosa
Daisy Family (Asteraceae). Native.
Blooms: August through November.
Habitat: Open prairies, fields and roadsides.
Flowers: Very small, yellow flower heads (large for Goldenrods) spirally arranged in a large spike-like cluster.
Leaves and Stem: Alternate, lance-shaped, pointed and toothed leaves.
Note: There are 13 goldenrods common along the Missouri River. They are difficult to tell apart. Though it is thought to cause hay fever, a goldenrod's pollen is too heavy to stay in the air.

BLUE - FEBRUARY

SMALL BLUETS
Hedyotis crassifolia (formerly *Houstionia pusilla*)
Madder Family (Rubiaceae). Native.
Blooms: February through April.
Habitat: Open areas of lawns, fields, prairies, glades and along roads. Often grow in mats.
Flowers: Tiny, deep blue or purple flower that looks skyward with 4 pointed petals.
Leaves and Stem: Tiny plant with narrow, opposite leaves and thread-like stem.
Note: One of the first signs of spring. This plant has more common names than any other Missouri plant.

BLUE - MARCH

JOHNNY-JUMP-UP
Also called Field Pansy or Wild Pansy
Viola rafinesquii
Violet Family (Violaceae). Native.
Blooms: March through May.
Habitat: Open areas in lawns, fields, glades and roadsides.
Flowers: Small, very pale blue, violet-shaped flower with light yellow or white center. Lower 3 petals have purple veins.
Leaves and Stem: Small plant with rounded leaves and associated teeth. Some leaves occur on the stem. Stipules are large and deeply cut.
Note: The earliest Violet to bloom in the spring. Will carpet an entire area with flowers.

Blue - Late March

COMMON VIOLET
Also called Meadow Violet or Butterfly Violet.
Viola sororia
Violet Family (Violaceae). Native.
Blooms: March through June. Also may bloom in October and November.
Habitat: Dry or moist woods.
Flowers: Violet-shaped, deep blue flowers. Petals have boat-shaped spur. Lower petals have purple veins. Side petals are bearded.
Leaves and Stem: Leaves and flowers on separate stalks. Leaves are heart-shaped with scalloped margins.
Note: Very common edible plant that is very high in vitamins A and C. Some parts of the plant can be used for salads, jellies, drinks or eaten raw.

BLUEBELLS
Also called Virginia Cowslip.
Mertensia virginica
Borage Family (Boraginaceae). Native.
Blooms: Late March through early June
Habitat: Moist rich bottomland woods on lower slopes, along streams. Often grow in large masses.
Flowers: Trumpet-shaped flowers hanging in loose cluster at top of stems. Pink at first, then turning blue.
Leaves and Stem: Large, smooth, bluish-green, oval leaves. Only member of the family in Missouri with no hairs on stems or leaves. Number of stems per clump increases each year.
Note: One of the most beautiful flowers of early spring. One of the most easily grown of all the wildflowers.

BLUE - APRIL

BIRD'S-FOOT VIOLET
Also called Hens and Roosters.
Viola pedata
Violet Family (Violaceae). Native.
Blooms: April through early June.
Habitat: Thin, rocky soil of open woods, prairies, glades and along roads. Prefers thin soil.
Flowers: Flowers with 2 color varieties. The "hen" color variety has all 5 petals pale blue. The "rooster" color variety has the 2 upper petals with deep purple velvet, and the lower 3 petals are pale blue. Center of flower is always orange.
Leaves and Stem: All leaves coming for base of plant.
Leaves are deeply divided into slender lobes like a "bird's foot."
Note: Used in children's game called "Hen and Rooster." This handsome wildflower will often cover large areas and is one of the best sights of spring.

BLUE-EYED MARY
Collinsia verna
Figwort Family (Scrophulariaceae). Native.
Blooms: April through June.
Habitat: Moist rich bottomland woods and slopes. Absent from northwestern counties.
Flowers: Bicolor flower with 2 white upper lobes and 3 bright blue lower lobes. The center lower lobe wraps around the stamens and pistils.
Leaves and Stem: Leaves are opposite and egg-shaped. Middle leaves are stemless and clasp to the stem.
Note: This plant forms dense carpets in springtime.

DWARF LARKSPUR
Delphinium tricorne
Buttercup Family (Ranunculaceae). Native.
Blooms: April through early June.
Habitat: Rich or rocky wooded slopes.
Flowers: Loose cluster of blue or violet 1 in.-long flowers with erect, long spur (upper sepal).
Leaves and Stem: Leaves are deeply divided into finger-like lobes. Short plant, typically 8–18 in.
Note: Plant is poisonous—one of the most common causes of cattle poisoning.

GROUND IVY
Also called Gill-Over-the-Ground.
Glechoma hederacea
Mint Family (Lamiaceae).
Introduced, native of Europe.
Blooms: April through July.
Habitat: In bottomland woods, along roads and around old dwellings.
Flowers: Blue or violet, mint-shaped flowers at base of leaves.
Leaves and Stem: Opposite, kidney shaped, bluntly toothed leaves. A low creeping square stem.
Note: An attractive ground cover plant that escaped from lawns and has become a problem plant. Spreads rapidly and is hard to eradicate because the creeping stems readily take root.

HAIRY VETCH
Vicia villosa
Pea Family (Fabaceae). Introduced, from Europe.
Blooms: April through October.
Habitat: Open fields and along roads. Often form large spreading mats.
Flowers: Many large, 1/2 in.-long, blue and white pea-like flowers on a long, one-sided spike.
Leaves and Stem: Leaf divided into a row of 6–8 pairs of leaflets. Leaf has a tendril at the end. Plant is hairy.
Note: A trailing plant that uses its tendrils to bind to other objects.

JACOB'S LADDER
Also called Greek Valerian.
Polemonium reptans
Phlox Family (Polemoniaceae). Native.
Blooms: April through June.
Habitat: Moist, wooded bottomlands and slopes.
Flowers: Loose cluster of light blue to violet-blue bell-shaped flowers with yellow stamens.
Leaves and Stem: Leaf divided into a ladder of paired smooth-edged leaflets.
Note: Native Americans used this plant medicinally to induce vomiting and promote sweating.

PRAIRIE BLUE-EYED GRASS
Sisyrinchium campestre
Iris Family (Iridaceae). Native.
Blooms: April through June.
Habitat: Prairies, glades, fields and open rocky woods.
Flowers: Small (1/2 in.-wide) blue flowers with yellow center and yellow stamens. The 6 petals are tipped with small bristles.
Leaves and Stem: Narrow, grass-like, stiff leaves that grows in clumps. Stem does not branch.
Note: A wildflower and not a grass.

WILD SWEET WILLIAM
Also called Blue Phlox.
Phlox divaricata
Phlox Family (Polemoniaceae). Native.
Blooms: April through June.
Habitat: Moist bottomland and open woods.
Flowers: Loose cluster of blue, lavender or light pink. Tubular flowers with the 5 lobes indented at tip and narrow at base.
Leaves and Stem: Opposite, lance-shaped leaves. Stem is hairy and sticky.
Note: These "sweet" smelling wildflowers cover our wooded bottomlands with color in the spring.

WILD HYACINTH
Camassia scilloides
Lily Family (Liliaceae). Native.
Blooms: April through mid-May.
Habitat: Limestone prairies, glades, rocky slopes and open woods. Absent from northwestern part of the Missouri River valley.
Flowers: Delicate and fragrant, 6 pointed flower of very pale blue color and 6 yellow-tipped stamens. As many as 15–40 flowers in long cylinder-like cluster. Flowers at base of stalk blooms first.
Leaves and Stem: Very narrow, grass-like leaves coming from underground bulb.
Note: Bulbs can be edible.

BLUE - MAY

LEAD PLANT
Amorpha canescens
Pea Family (Fabaceae). Native.
Blooms: May through August.
Habitat: Dry prairies, glades and fields.
Flowers: Tiny, lavender-colored, pea-shaped flowers in a dense spike with yellow, protruding stamens.
Leaves and Stem: Leaves divided into 15–25 gray, hairy, rounded leaflets in a pinnate arrangement. Shrubby plant with dense gray hairs.
Note: Called the Lead Plant because of its gray, hairy appearance and because it was thought to grow on top of lead deposits.

OHIO SPIDERWORT
Tradescantia ohiensis
Spiderwort Family (Commelinaceae). Native.
Blooms: May through July.
Habitat: Prairies, fields and roadsides.
Flowers: Cluster of bright blue or purple flowers with 3 broad petals and yellow stamens with blue hairs.
Leaves and Stem: Long, narrow and grass-like leaves. Tall (2–3 ft.), branching plant. Plant is not hairy.
Note: Does this plant remind you of a spider? The hairs on the stamens turn pink in the present of too much ozone pollution.

COMMON DAYFLOWER
Also called the Asiatic Dayflower.
Commelina communis
Spiderwort Family (Commelinaceae). Native of Asia.
Blooms: May through October
Habitat: Moist, shaded bottomland woods, old dwellings and other disturbed areas.
Flowers: A 1 in.-wide flower with 2 large, blue, ear-like petals above and 1 tiny white petal below.
Leaves and Stem: Alternate, lance-shaped and clasping leaves. Has a weak stem that often topples over and rots at the joints.
Note: Each flower lasts for only a single day. Plant is used medicinally in China.

BLUE — LATE MAY

WILD BERGAMONT
Also called Horsemint.
Monarda fistulosa
Mint Family (Lamiaceae). Native.
Blooms: Late May through August.
Habitat: Open dry areas in prairies, fields and along roads.
Flowers: A dense head or cluster of large, 1 in.-long, pink or lilac, tubular flowers, with protruding stamens.
Leaves and Stem: Opposite (paired), lance-shaped and toothed leaves. Stem is square.
Note: The illustration shows Bee Balm, a related species, but less common near the river. A tea from Horsemint leaves was used medicinally by Native Americans and settlers to treat colds and the flu. Contains the chemical thymol, an antiseptic.

COMMON CHICKORY
Also called Blue Sailors.
Cichorium intybus
Daisy Family (Asteraceae). Introduced, native of Europe.
Blooms: Late May through October.
Habitat: Open fields and along roads.
Flowers: Bright blue, stalkless flower head that has square rays tipped with sharp teeth. Flowers become whitish with age.
Leaves and Stem: The upper stem has few leaves. Lower leaves are deeply lobed and dandelion-like.
Note: The roots can be used as a coffee substitute.

BLUE — JUNE

BULL THISTLE
Cirsium vulgare
Daisy Family (Asteraceae).
Introduced, native of Europe.
Blooms: June through September.
Habitat: Fields, along roads and other disturbed areas.
Flowers: Large, dense flower head of purple flowers. Yellow spines on the flower bracts just below the flower heads.
Leaves and Stem: Alternate leaves that are deeply lobed, hairy and spiny. Whole plant is very prickly.
Note: Goldfinches are fond of the seeds of thistles. Thistle flowers were used by settlers to curdle milk.

MAD-DOG SKULLCAP
Scutellaria lateriflora
Mint Family (Lamiaceae). Native.
Blooms: June through October.
Habitat: Wet or moist bottomland woods, gravel bars along streams and bases of bluffs.
Flowers: Small, violet-blue, lipped and hooded flowers in a one-sided cluster coming from the base of the leaves.
Leaves and Stem: Opposite (paired), egg-shaped and coarsely toothed leaves with stalks. The stem is square.
Note: Common name comes from the belief that the plant could cure rabies and act as a nerve tonic.

BLUE - JULY

GREEN-STEMMED JOE-PYE WEED
Also called the Sweet Joe-Pye Weed.
Eupatorium purpureum
Daisy Family (Asteraceae). Native.
Blooms: July through September
Habitat: Wet bottomlands and moist wooded slopes.
Flowers: Small, pale, pink or purple flower heads in a large, dome-shaped, branching cluster.
Leaves and Stem: Lance-shaped and toothed leaves in whorls of 3 or 4. Stem is green with purple at leaf joints. Plant omits the scent of vanilla when bruised.
Note: Was used medicinally to treat kidney ailments. This plant, like all of the other *Eupatorium,* is usually avoided by grazing animals.

BLUE - AUGUST

BLUE CARDINAL FLOWER
Lobelia siphilitica
Bellflower Family (Campanulaceae). Native.
Blooms: August through October.
Habitat: Wet bottomland woods and along streams, ponds and roadside ditches.
Flowers: A tall spike of large (1 in.), blue, tubular flowers with two narrow, upper lips and 3 wide, lower lips. White stripes under lower lobes.
Leaves and Stem: Alternate, lance-shaped and toothed leaves. Plant grows up to 3 ft. tall.
Note: Used by Native Americans for the treatment of syphilis and colds. **May be poisonous**.

ROUGH BLAZING STAR
Also called Gay Feather.
Liatris aspera
Daisy Family (Asteraceae). Native.
Blooms: August through November.
Habitat: Dry open prairies, glades, fields and roadsides.
Flowers: Many rose-purple, button-shaped flower heads with short stalks on a long spike. Flower heads supported by rounded bracts that angle outward.
Leaves and Stem: Very narrow, alternate leaves on tall plants.
Note: Most common of the 5 blazing stars along the Missouri River. Used medicinally by settlers to treat kidney problems.

RED – FEBRUARY

HENBIT
Lamium amplexicaule
Mint Family (Lamiaceae). Native of Europe, Asia.
Blooms: February through November.
Habitat: Open fields, roadsides and railbeds.
Flowers: Bright lavender, erect flowers with red spots on lips. Flowers in cluster at top of plant.
Leaves and Stem: Leaves are rounded with blunt teeth. Upper leaves lack stems and encircle the central stem. As in all mints, the stem is square.
Note: Forms carpets of color in early spring. Does not have the scent of most mints. Birds love seeds.

RED – MARCH

ROSE VERVAIN
Also called Rose Verbena or Eastern Verbena.
Glandularia candensis (formerly *Verbena candensis)*
Vervain Family (Verbenaceae). Native.
Blooms: March through November.
Habitat: Glades, bluffs, prairies, open rocky woodlands and roadsides.
Flowers: Rose-colored tubular flowers with 5 flaring lobes with notched ends. Flowers are in dense rounded clusters at top of stem.

Leaves and Stem: Leaves are deeply lobed and sharply toothed. Each plant has several hairy stems.

Note: Flowers are very fragrant. Best known and most showy of all the other plants in its family.

RED - APRIL

SHOOTING STAR
Dodecatheon meadia
Primrose Family (Primulaceae). Native.
Blooms: April through June.
Habitat: Glades, bluffs, prairies and open rocky woods.
Flowers: The pink, lavender or white petals curve backwards, while the 5 yellow stamens point downward. Nodding flowers in cluster on leafless stem.
Leaves and Stem: At the base of plant are the large, lance-shaped leaves with reddish stalks.
Note: Pollinated by bees. One of the more beautiful and graceful spring wildflowers.

WILD COLUMBINE
Aquilegia canadensis
Buttercup Family (Ranunculaceae). Native.
Blooms: April through July.
Habitat: Limestone bluffs, rocky ledges and slopes.
Flowers: Five bright red, upward-pointing hollow spurs with ball at end and yellow tips at the bottom. Numerous stamens hang below the petals. Flowers hang downward nodding at the end of the stem.
Leaves and Stem: Light green leaves are divided into 3 deeply lobed leaflets.
Note: Spurs contain nectar that attracts long-tongued insects. Used by Native Americans as a perfume and love charm. **Plant may be poisonous.**

WILD GERANIUM
Also called Spotted Cranesbill.
Geranium maculatum
Geranium Family (Geraniaceae). Native.
Blooms: April through June.
Habitat: Rich or rocky open woods.
Flowers: Several pink or lavender, 1 in.-wide flowers with 5 petals. Long, pointed fruit resembles the bill of a crane.
Leaves and Stem: Large (3–6 in.), opposite, 5–7 deeply lobbed leaves. Grows to 2 ft. tall.
Note: Used by Native Americans and settlers to stop bleeding and treat illnesses.

RED - MAY

CROWN VETCH
Securigera varia (formerly *Coronilla varia*)
Pea Family (Fabaceae).
Introduced, native of Europe, Asia and Africa.
Blooms: May through August.
Habitat: Fields and along roads.
Flowers: Clover-like cluster of pink and white pea-shaped flowers.
Leaves and Stem: Alternate leaves divided into many small, paired leaflets. A creeping plant.
Note: Planted by the Missouri Highway Department as ground cover for steep banks.

PALE-PURPLE CONEFLOWER
Echinacea pallida
Daisy Family (Asteraceae). Native.
Blooms: May through July.
Habitat: Dry prairies, fields, limestone glades and roadsides.
Flowers: A large, daisy-like flower with drooping, slender pale purple rays and a brown, cone-like head.
Leaves and Stem: Lower leaves are long-stalked, lance-shaped, parallel veined and without teeth. Stem leaves are smaller with shorter stalks. Plant is 3 ft. tall and stem has spreading hairs.
Note: Native Americans used this plant and the Purple Coneflower (*Echinacea purpurea*) frequently as medicine.

PASTURE ROSE
Rosa carolina
Rose Family (Rosaceae). Native.
Blooms: May through June.
Habitat: Moist prairies, fields and thickets.
Flowers: Large, 3 in.-wide, 3-petaled pink flower. Smells very good.
Leaves and Stem: Leaves divided into 3, 5 or 7 sharply-toothed, dull green leaflets. A bushy plant (grows up to 7 ft. high) with straight, slender thorns.
Note: This plant and the Prairie Rose are two of the most beautiful of our native roses. Also, the most common of the native roses.

RED CLOVER
Trifolium pratense
Pea Family (Fabaceae). Introduced, native of Europe.
Blooms: May through September.
Habitat: Open areas in fields, pastures and roadsides.
Flowers: Red to reddish-purple flower that forms dense, round heads.
Leaves and Stem: Divided into 3 large oval leaflets each with a light V-shaped design. Hairy stems.
Note: One of the most important forage crops in the United States. Red Clover tea has been used medicinally. Diseased clover has an alkaloid that is being studied as a potential AIDS and diabetes treatment.

SHEEP SORREL
Also called Red Sorrel or Field Sorrel.
Rumex acetosella
Smartweed Family (Polygonaceae).
Native of Europe.
Blooms: May through September. Bears fruit June through October
Habitat: Open, dry disturbed areas and fields.
Flowers: Tiny, green flowers in long, branching clusters. The flowers often turn brownish red.
Leaves and Stem: Small, alternate, arrow-shaped leaves with spreading lobes. Stems are jointed.
Note: Sour tasting leaves were used as a thirst-quencher and in salads. **May be poisonous.**

RED - LATE MAY

BUTTERFLY WEED
Also called Chigger Weed.
Asclepias tuberosa
Milkweed Family (Asclepiadaceae).
Native.
Blooms: Late May through September.
Habitat: Open, dry or rocky prairies, glades, fields and roadsides.
Flowers: Small bright orange to red, milkweed-like flowers in a flat-topped cluster.
Leaves and Stem: Alternate, narrow, lance-shaped leaves without stalks. Stem is hairy and lacks the milky juice of other milkweeds.
Note: Early settlers thought this plant was the source of chiggers.

COMMON MILKWEED
Asclepias syriaca
Milkweed Family (Asclepiadaceae).
Native.
Blooms: Late May through August.
Habitat: Fields, prairies, glades and along roads.
Flowers: A dome-shaped cluster of small, very fragrant, pink to purple flowers with horns that curve back. Seeds with fluffy fibers in a large, warty seedpod.
Leaves and Stem: Opposite, egg-shaped leaves with fine hairs underneath. Thick, milk-like juice present in stem and leaves.
Note: Releasing the seeds from their

seedpod and watching them float through the air brings out the kid in all of us. This is the most abundant variety of the 12 milkweeds that grow in the valley.

IRONWEED
Vernonia baldwinii
Daisy Family (Asteraceae). Native.
Blooms: Late May through September.
Habitat: Prairies, fields, glades and along roads.
Flowers: Many small flower heads, 1/2 in.-wide, each with many (up to 35) small purple flowers. The bracts below the flower heads are pointed.
Leaves and Stem: Large, alternate, hairy and toothed leaves that are pointed at both ends. Tall plants, many grow 3–4 ft. high.
Note: Most common of the 5 species along the River. Called Ironweed, because of their durable nature.

PRAIRIE ROSE
Rosa setigera
Rose Family (Rosaceae). Native.
Blooms: Late May through July.
Habitat: Moist, prairies, fields and thickets.
Flowers: Large, 3 in.-wide, 5-petaled pink flower in a small cluster. Smells great.
Leaves and Stem: Leaves divided into 3 sharply toothed, shinny leaflets. Stem is a long (up to 12 ft.) arching or climbing cane with curved, well-spaced thorns.

Note: This plant and the Pasture Rose are the most beautiful of our native roses. The leaves turn a deep red color in the fall.

SENSITIVE BRIER
Schrankia nuttallii
Mimosa Family (Mimosaceae). Native.
Blooms: Late May to September.
Habitat: Prairies and woods.
Flowers: Small pink to rose-colored tubular flowers with protruding yellow stamens in a round, ball-shaped flower head.
Leaves and Stem: Doubly divided

leaves that are divided into leaflets. Each leaflet is further divided into other tiny leaflets. Stem bears many curved thorns. Plant creeps along the ground.
Note: When the leaves are touched they immediately fold up making this our most "sensitive" native plant.

COMMON SMARTWEED
Also called Pinkweed
or Pennsylvania Smartweed.
Polygonum pensylvanicum
Smartweed Family (Polygonaceae). Native.
Blooms: May though October
Habitat: Wet, open, bottomland areas.
Flowers: Very small rose-pink flowers in a
dense, thick spike. Many flower spikes per plant.
Leaves and Stem: Alternate, lance-shaped,
smooth-edged, long pointed, shiny leaves. Stem
has reddish joints. Upper stem has tiny hair-like
glands.
Note: Native American used the plant medici-
nally. **Fresh juice may cause skin irritation.**
Common along our streams in the summer. One
of four Smartweeds along the Missouri River.

RED – JUNE

BOUNCING BET
Also called Soapwort.
Saponaria officinalis
Pink Family (Caryophyllaceae). Native of Europe.
Blooms: June through October.
Habitat: Gravel and sandbars along streams, fields
and roadsides. Often grow in large colonies.
Flowers: Dense cluster of fragrant pink or white,
long, tubular flowers. Petals often curl back and
are notched at tip.
Leaves and Stem: Opposite, lance-shaped leaves.
Stem is thick-jointed. Stem and leaves do not have
hair. Plant is typically 1–2 ft. tall.
Note: When mixed with water, the juice of this
plant forms a lather you can use to wash your hands.

WINGED LOOSESTRIFE
Lythrum alatum
Loosestrife Family (Lythraceae). Native
Blooms: Early June through September.
Habitat: In wetlands and margins of ponds.
Flowers: Small, 1/2 in.-wide, pink or purple 6-petaled flowers located at the base of the leaves.
Leaves and Stem: Lance-shaped, dark green leaves, with lower leaves being opposite or in a whorl of 3, with some of the upper leaves being alternate. Stem is 4-sided and may be winged.
Note: A nasty relative of this plant, the introduced Purple Loosestrife (*Lythrum salicaria*), invades wetlands and eliminates the native flora. It should be removed from all wetlands in Missouri.

BROWN - APRIL

JACK-IN-THE-PULPIT
Also called Indian Turnip
Arisaema triphyllum
Arum Family (Araceae). Native.
Blooms: April through June.
Habitat: Rich moist woods.
Flowers: The pale green striped with purplish brown hood (the "Pulpit") curves over the club-like flower stalk (the "Jack"). The tiny flowers are at the base of the flower stalk. In the fall the fruit is a dense cluster of bright-red berries.
Leaves and Stem: One, 3-divided, dull green leaf coming out of the base.
Note: Fresh plants are poisonous if eaten raw. Native Americans dried the roots to make flour. The plant sometimes has both male and female flowers.

WAKE ROBIN TRILLIUM
Trillium sessile
Lilly Family (Liliaceae). Native.
Blooms: Early April through early June.
Habitat: Lower slopes of rich moist woods, along streams or bluffs.
Flowers: The single reddish-brown or maroon flower with 3 narrow, erect petals pointing skyward. Flower arising from center of 3 sepals and 3 leaves without a stalk.
Leaves and Stem: Three leaves, without stalk, in a whorl just below the flower, giving the appearance of a 3-pointed star.
Each leaf is dark green and may be mottled with white and green areas.
Note: Called Wake Robin from the folklore legend that their flowering would wake up the robins after winter hibernation.

WILD GINGER
Asarum canadense
Birthwort Family
(Aristolochiaceae). Native.
Blooms: April through May.
Habitat: Rich, moist woods.
Flowers: Single reddish-brown, cup-shaped, 3-lobbed, hairy flower found hidden at the base of leaves.
Leaves and Stem: Two large rounded heart-shaped leaves. Root with strong taste and smell of ginger.
Note: Flowers smells like decaying fruit and are polli-

nated by ground insects. Roots were used as a ginger substitute. Used medicinally by Native Americans. Plant contains tumor-inhibiting compound.

Vines, Canes & Rushes

White - April

BLACK RASPBERRY
Rubus occidentalis
Rose Family (Rosaceae).
Native.
Blooms: April through June and fruits June through July. Plant usually occurs in large colonies.
Habitat: Open woods, fields and along roads.
Flowers: Small, 1/2 in.-wide white, 5-petaled flowers. Fruit is purplish-black.
Leaves and Stem: Leaves divided into 3 or 5 toothed leaflets that are white below. The round, purple stems have a white coating that can be rubbed off. Stems also have curved thorns. An arching vine may root from the tip.
Note: One of the first to ripen and the sweetest of the edible summer berries. The leaves were used in medicinal teas. This plant is virtually identical to the Dewberry and Blackberry plants, except for the color of its berries.

BLACKBERRY
Also called the High-Bush Blackberry.
Rubus pensilvanicus
Rose Family (Rosaceae). Native.
Blooms: April through June. Fruits June through August.
Habitat: Open woods, prairies, fields and along roads. Occur in large colonies.
Flowers: White, 1 in.-wide, 5-petaled flowers. Fruit is black.
Leaves and Stem: Leaves are divided into 5 (also 3 or 7) toothed leaflets. The thorny, angular, brown stem forms an arching vine.
Note: The most commonly picked and used summer berry in Missouri. The berry is great eaten raw or in pies. Watch the thorns!

DEWBERRY
Rubus flagellaris
Rose Family (Rosaceae). Native.
Blooms: April through June and fruits June through August.
Habitat: Open prairies, fields and along roads.
Flowers: Bright white, 3/4 in.-wide, 5-petaled flower. Fruit is similar to the black-berry but fewer and larger.
Leaves and Stem: A creeping, thorny vine with leaves divided into 3 or 5 leaf-lets. Topmost leaflet is broadest near bottom. The related blackberry is a more erect plant.
Note: The fruit is very tasty and can be used the same as the related blackberry. The plants and berries are important wildlife foods.

MISSOURI GOOSEBERRY
Also called Wild Gooseberry.
Ribes missouriense
Currant Family (Grossulariaceae). Native.
Blooms: April and May. Fruits June through September
Habitat: Open upland or bottom-land wood and fields.
Flowers: Small, greenish-white, bell-shaped flowers with long sta-mens and pistils. Flowers hanging down under stems. Fruit is first green, then turns black.
Leaves and Stem: Woody shrub with red thorns. Alternate leaves are deeply lobed and as broad as long, on a long stem.
Note: One of the first woody plants to produce leaves in the spring. The green fruit can be used in the famous Missouri Gooseberry Pie.

WHITE - MAY

FIELD BINDWEED
Convolvulus arvensis
Morning Glory Family
(Convolvulaceae).
Introduced, native of
Europe and Asia.
Blooms: May through
September.
Habitat: Open fields and
along roads.
Flowers: White or light
pink, small (3/4 in.-long),
funnel-shaped flowers.

Leaves and Stem: Alternate, arrow-shaped leaves with sharp lobes at base. Creeping or climbing vines forming dense mats.
Note: Medicinally used for spider bites. This plant may become a problem because the colony can cover many areas.

JAPANESE HONEYSUCKLE
Lonicera japonica
Honeysuckle Family (Caprifoliaceae).
Introduced, native of Asia.
Blooms: May and June
Habitat: Open woods, thickets, fencerows and along roads.
Flowers: White or yellow, tubular flowers with long, curved stamens. Fruit is a
blue-black berry.
Leaves and Stem: Opposite (paired) egg-
shaped leaves with short stem. Lower
leaves are often lobed. A weedy vine
which can cover large areas.
Note: This plant has escaped from culti-
vation and strangles small native trees and
shrubs. It is a very severe threat to our
native plants and natural areas.

MULTIFLORA ROSE
Also called Japanese Rose.
Rosa multiflora
Rose Family (Roasaceae).
Introduced, native of Japan.
Blooms: May and June.
Habitat: Open areas of fields, pastures and along roads.
Flowers: Clusters of numerous, small, white and 5-petaled flowers.
Leaves and Stem: Alternate leaves divided into 7 to 9 leaflets. A shrub with long, arching stems.
Note: Was introduced to Missouri to be used as a "living fence," but has spread throughout the area and is now a big problem. Birds love to eat the bright red fruit of this plant.

WHITE - LATE MAY

WILD POTATO VINE
Also called Man-of-the-Earth.
Ipomoea pandurata
Morning Glory Family (Convolvulaceae). Native.
Blooms: Late May through September.
Habitat: Bottomland fields, pastures and along roads.
Flowers: Large, trumpet-shaped, white flowers with pink stripes in throat.
Leaves and Stem: Heart-shaped and smooth edged leaves. A purple-stemmed, climbing vine which may get 15 ft. long.
Note: The huge root, which grows straight down, may be up to 2 ft. long and weigh several pounds. Root was used medicinally by Native Americans.
The roots may be poisonous.

BLUE - JULY

BLUE MORNING GLORY
Also called Ivy-Leaved Morning Glory.
Ipomoea hederacea
Morning Glory Family (Convolvulaceae).
Introduced, native of South America.
Blooms: July through October.
Habitat: Open fields, along roads and other disturbed areas.
Flowers: Blue or purple trumpet-shaped flower. Sepals have long, narrow tips.
Leaves and Stem: Leaves with 3 deep lobes and heart-shaped base. Stem and leaves are hairy, a distinctive vine.
Note: Introduced from South America.

RED - MAY

TRUMPET CREEPER
Also called Devil's Shoe Laces.
Campsis radicans
Trumpet Creeper Family (Bignoniaceae). Native.
Blooms: May through August.
Habitat: Open areas of woods, thickets, old fields, bluffs and along roads.
Flowers: Large (3 in.), reddish-orange, trumpet-shaped, 5-lobed in a cluster.
Leaves and Stem: Opposite leaves divided into 7–11 sharply toothed leaflets. High climbing woody vine without tendrils.
Note: The bright orange-red flowers are very popular with hummingbirds.
Warning! Some people get a poison-Ivy type rash after touching the plant.

Brown - Late May

COMMON CAT-TAIL
Typha latifolia
Cat-Tail Family (Typhaceae). Native.
Blooms: Late May through July.
Habitat: Wetlands and muddy margins of pond and streams in large colonies.
Flowers: Brownish flowers in dense 1 in.-wide cylindrical spike. Upper part of the spike has male flowers and the lower part of the spike has female flowers. Spike resembles a tail of a cat. Both parts of the spike touch each other.
Leaves and Stem: Long, grass-like, 1 in.-wide, stiff and bluish- or grayish-green.
Note: One of the most useful plants for Native Americans. The leaves were woven into floor mats and other items, the roots are edible, and the down from the mature spikes were used like cotton diapers.

Green - May

AMERICAN BITTERSWEET
Celastrus scandens
Staff Tree Family (Celastraceae). Native.
Blooms: May and June, fruits July to October
Habitat: Woods, along bluffs, glades, thickets and fencerows.
Flowers: Small greenish flowers in clusters. Fruit is very ornamental with orange pods splitting to reveal scarlet seeds.
Leaves and Stem: Alternate, egg-shaped and wavy-toothed leaves. A high climbing or tangled vine without tendrils. Leaves turns pale yellow in fall.
Note: Over-collection for its ornamental fruits has virtually wiped out this plant.

BRISTLY GREENBRIER
Also called Catbrier.

Smilax hispida

Greenbrier Family (Smilacaceae). Native.

Blooms: May and June.

Habitat: Bottomland woods and fields.

Flowers: Round cluster of tiny green flowers on long flower stem. Fruit is black.

Leaves and Stem: Heart-shaped leaves with parallel veins. A green-stemmed, climbing vine with tendrils and bristles.

Note: One of the few woody, green and thorny vines in Missouri. A close encounter with this plant can leave scars. Plant was used medicinally by Native Americans to relieve pain.

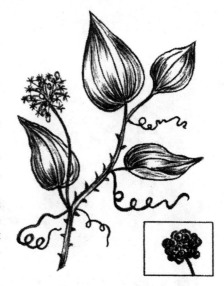

GRAYBARK GRAPE
Also called the Sweet Winter Grape or the Pigeon Grape.

Vitis cinerea

Grape Family (Vitaceae). Native.

Blooms: May through July. Fruits from September through October.

Habitat: Bottomland woods and thickets.

Flowers: Clusters of small greenish flowers which are either males or females. The sweet, ripe fruit is black.

Leaves and Stem: Alternate, shallow-lobed leaves with gray hairs on lower surface. Twigs also have gray hairs. A high climbing vine with tendrils.

Note: The most common of the eight species of wild grapes in Missouri. Can be confused with the Virginia Creeper or Poison Ivy. Does not have the compound leaves of the Virginia Creeper or the hairy vine and 3 leaves of Poison Ivy. The German-Americans crossed the wild grapes of Missouri with the cultivated grapes to produce the famous Norton Grape.

POISON IVY

Toxicodendron radicans
(formerly *Rhus radicans*)
Cashew Family (Anacardiaceae). Native.
Blooms: May through July. Fruits August through November.
Habitat: In many habitats such as woodlands woods, bluffs, along roads and fencerows.
Flowers: Green and very small (1/8 in.) in small branching clusters. Fruit is gray or white.
Leaves and Stem: Alternate leaves divided into 3 leaflets, the middle leaflet with a much longer stem. A woody plant that can be a climbing vine or an erect shrub. The stem of the climbing vine has many short aerial rootlets, which gives it a hairy appearance.
Note: Try to avoid contact with this plant. **It has a volatile oil which is a dangerous skin irritant.** After contact, many people develop a skin rash in a few hours or a few days. After any contact, wash skin with soap in hot water. **To be safe remember "leaves of 3 let it be."** Remember many trees in the woods have a poison ivy vine on them. The plant is eaten by deer, and many birds like the fruit.

GREEN — LATE MAY

VIRGINIA CREEPER

Also called Woodbine or Five-Leaved Ivy.
Parthenocissus quinquefolia
Grape Family (Vitaceae). Native.
Blooms: Late May through August.
Habitat: Bottomland woods, bluffs and fencerows.
Flowers: Small and greenish or whitish in branching clusters. Berries are bluish-black.
Leaves and Stem: Divided into 5, toothed leaflets in a fan-shape. A woody vine with long, slender tendrils, ending in a cup-like disk.
Note: The only vine in Missouri with fan-shaped leaves and cup-shaped tendrils. The berries are an important wildlife food. The leaves turn a brilliant red in the fall.

Plants With Stickers, Burs, Seeds or Other Parts That Can Stick to You

BEDSTRAW
Galium aparine
Size: From 2 to 6 ft. Often trailing.
Flower: White to yellow, 1/8 in., flowers in open clusters at branch tops.
Blooms: April through July.
Leaves: Small, lance-shaped, bristly, and in whorls along stems.
Where to find: In open places, along rail beds, moist or rich thickets and woodlands.
Note: Another variety is known for its sweet fragrance. Used to make mattresses by early settlers. Will stick to your clothing. Breaks off easily.

STINGING NETTLE
Laportea canadensis
Size: From 2 to 4 ft. Upper portion of stem is hairy.
Flower: Long slender clusters at top of plant and among the leaves.
Blooms: June through August.
Leaves: Triangular, paired, toothed, and covered with stinging hairs.
Where to find: Edges of woods, hills and bottomlands.
Note: The stinging hairs break off easily and produce intense irritation for several minutes.

TICK TREFOIL

Desmodium glutinosum
Size: From 3 to 4 ft.
Hairy stems, sometimes trails.
Flower: Pea-shaped, rose purple to magenta in tall loose spikes on long stems with no leaves.
Blooms: June through August.
Leaves: Divided, egg-shaped and pointed at ends, middle leaf of the 3 is the longest.
Where to find: Open rocky woods, valleys and clearings.
Note: Also called Beggar's Lice. Seedpods are hairy and stick to clothing.

STICKTIGHTS

Biden frondosa
Size: From 1 to 4 ft.
Flower: Yellow, button-like with ray-shaped petals. Seeds have barbed prongs.
Blooms: August through October.
Leaves: Lance-shaped, toothed, opposite and in pairs.
Where to find: Wet places and stream banks.
Note: Also called Beggar-Ticks.

COCKLEBUR

Xanthium spinosum
Size: From 1 to 6 ft. Bushy plant.
Flower: Flower heads are greenish. Burs are dark brown, egg-shaped, prickly.
Blooms: August through October.
Leaves: Toothed, lobed and oval to wedge-shaped.
Where to find: Fields and disturbed areas.
Note: Do not let your pet get near this plant! Their hair will get matted with these Cockleburs.

Two Premier Missouri Prairie Grasses

Nearly 200 years ago, much of Missouri was blanketed in native tallgrass prairies. These regions, which supported an abundance of wild grasses, wildflowers and other forms of wildlife, virtually disappeared from our landscape following settlement. Today, as more people have come to value the beauty, diversity and ecological importance of tallgrass prairies, reconstructed prairies have become more common. The following two entries, Big Blue Stem and Little Blue Stem, are premier grasses of the tallgrass prairies and deserve special attention.

BIG BLUE STEM
Andropogon gerardit
Size: From 2 to 8 ft.
Flower: Forked lavender to bronze purple, spikelets with long gray or silver hairs.
Blooms: July through October.
Leaves: Ribbon-like, often drooping stems, from base.
Where to find: Prairies and fields.
Note: Also called Turkey Foot.

LITTLE BLUE STEM
Andropogon scoparius
Size: From 1 to 4 ft.
Flower: Creamy stubby spikes covered with long hairy prongs.
Blooms: July through October.
Leaves: Long and narrow from base.
Where to find: Prairies and fields.
Note: Also called Broom Grass or Beardgrass.

Ferns & Related Plants

F erns are plants that reproduce by spores usually found on the stalks or on the underside of the leaflets. They generally need to be close to water and commonly grow in moist soils. Fronds—or fern leaves (including the stems)—may be undivided, divided once, divided into leaflets or lobed.

A Sample Entry for Ferns & Related Plants

COMMON NAME
Scientific Name
Family Name—Native or Non-Native.
Habitat: Soil preferences and distribution.
Spores: Spore maturation and position.
Leaves: Includes size, shape and orientation.
Stalk: Identifying colors, description and features.
Note: Other common names, interesting facts or trivia.

Common Identification Terms

Fruit Dots or Sori – Masses of spore cases or sporangia that are sacks which contains the spores.

Stalk – The stem that supports the leaves.

Leaf or Frond – The flat, green, food-producing part of the fern.

Leaflets or Blade – Divisions of the leaves.

Spore – Simple reproductive bodies of ferns that consist of a single cell. After dispersion spores will become new ferns.

HORSETAILS
Also called Winter Scouring Rush
Equisetum hyemale
Horsetail Family (Equisetaceae). Native.
Habitat: Moist bottomland areas along streams. Occurs in dense colonies.
Spores: March through August. Borne on a short, black stem at top of plant.
Stem: A tall (3 ft. or more), evergreen plant with jointed stem and no leaves. The stem is rough because of ridges and the joints are black.
Note: This plant is related to the ferns and is one of Missouri's most primitive plants. Three hundred million years ago, during the Pennsylvanian Period, Missouri was covered with forests of giant, tree-sized horsetails and ferns. The rough stem has been used for scouring pots and as sandpaper. There are 4 other *Equisetum* which occur within the valley.

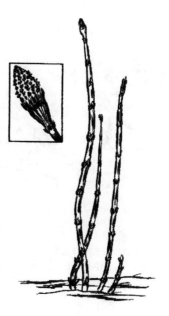

CHRISTMAS FERN
Polystichum acrostichoides
Wood Fern Family (Dryopteridaceae). Native.
Habitat: Dry or moist wooded slopes and ravines, especially on north-facing slopes.
Spores: Spores mature from June through October. Many round, red-brown fruit dots in rows on underside of the leaflets.
Leaves: Large (3 ft.), dark green leaves are divided into many opposite (paired), lance-shaped leaflets with an ear-like lobe at its base. The leaves remain green throughout the winter.
Stalk: The brown and green stalk is covered with scales.
Note: Gets its name from the fact that the fern is still green at Christmas. One of the most commonly encountered and easily recognized ferns in Missouri.

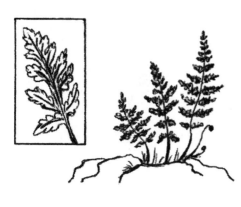

FRAGILE FERN
Also called Lowland Brittle Fern
Cystopteris protrusa
Wood Fern Family (Dryopteridaceae).
Native.

Habitat: Moist shaded recesses of limestone and sandstone bluffs, rich bottomland woods and ravines.

Spores: Spores mature June through September. Round cup-like fruit dots on underside of leaves.

Leaves: Small (10 in.), bright green, delicate and lance-shaped with long pointed tips. Divided into 12 pairs of deeply cut leaflets. Leaves die in winter.

Stalk: Shorter than the leaves. Stalk is brittle and will easily broken off. Base of stalk is brown or black and green above.

Note: This delicate fern gets its name from its brittle stalk. This fern will often die down to the ground during the summer only to reappear in the fall.

SENSITIVE FERN
Onoclea sensibilis
Wood Fern Family (Dryopteridaceae). Native.

Habitat: Wet bottomland woods and along streams.

Spores: Spores mature from June through November. Spores are borne in hard beads at the end of a separate 1 ft.-tall, branched, spike that becomes dark brown when mature.

Leaves: Two feet tall, leathery, broad and sturdy. Leave are not fern-like and divided into 12 pairs of leaflets. Leaflets with wavy margins. Lowest leaflets longer and separated from upper.

Stalk: Reddish-brown and green.

Note: Gets its name from the leaves being sensitive to frost and cold weather, after which it quickly dies, leaving the spore spike to winter.

PURPLE CLIFF BRAKE

Pellaea atropurpurea

Maidenhair Fern Family (Adiantaceae). Native.

Habitat: On dry limestone bluffs cracks and crevices.

Spores: Spores mature from April through September. Fruit dots are on the underside of the leaves along the margins.

Leaves: Stiff, wiry ferns with grayish blue-green, evergreen leaves. Divided into lance-shaped and smooth-edged leaflets.

Stalk: Stalk is purple-brown, wiry and hairy.

Note: This hardy little fern grows right on the face of bluffs where it seems to need very little soil.

NORTHERN MAIDENHAIR FERN

Adiantum pedatum

Maidenhair Fern Family (Adiantaceae). Native.

Habitat: Moist wooded slopes and ravine bottoms.

Spores: Spores mature from June through August. White to yellowish- green fruit dots on upper margins of the leaflets.

Leaves: Bluish-green, horizontal leaves arranged in a circular fan shape. Leaves divided into 5 or 6 long, curving leaflets. The leaflets are divided into long paired row of fan-shaped subleaftets.

Stalk: Long, black, smooth stalk, which becomes forked, then curves in opposite directions.

Note: One of our most beautiful ferns.

RATTLESNAKE FERN
Botrychium virginianum
Adders Tongue Family.
(Ophioglossaceae). Native.
Habitat: Woods.
Spores: Spores mature from May through July. Spores are in branching, yellow cluster on the end of a spike coming out of base of the leaf.
Leaves: Bright green, lacy, triangular and horizontal leaf. Leaf divided into egg-shaped, sharply-toothed leaflets. Leaves die in the early fall.
Stalk: Long (1 ft.) stalk ends at junction of the leaf and spore spike.
Note: The spore-bearing spike is the rattle of this Rattlesnake Fern.

WALKING FERN
Asplenium rhizophyllum
Spleenwort Family. (Aspleniaceae). Native.
Habitat: On moist, mossy, sheltered limestone or dolomite ledges, bluffs and boulders.
Spores: Spores mature from May through October. The brown fruit dots are scattered over the entire surface of the underside of the leaf.
Leaves: A single unfern-like, simple, evergreen leaf that is long and lance-shaped, tapering to a fine point, with a heart-shaped base. Often with tiny new plants at tips.
Stalk: Short, flattened and brown at the base and green above.
Note: This unusual fern sprouts a new plant wherever its tip touches soil. That is how it "walks" across the mossy rocks.

BIRDS

ird-watching, commonly called birding, is a favorite nature activity for many people. The Missouri River valley is home to a wide variety of birds. Over 400 different types of birds are known to visit our state each year. The Mississippi Flyway (a natural highway for birds formed by the Mississippi River) draws migrating species into the state from all ranges of North America.

The study of the different species and their habits can add substantial pleasure to any nature outing.

Birding is indeed both a hobby and a science. Ornithologists (bird scientists) have devoted their professional lives to the study of these feathered creatures. Although one doesn't need to become a professional to learn to identify many birds, a few important tips from the pros would be good to keep in mind:

- Spring and fall are often the best times to view the largest numbers of birds. In the spring, birds often display their most brilliant colors and migration brings many new species into the area. Fall also provides another chance to view native and migrating species; though their colorings are not usually as bright or distinctive.

- Sunrise to mid-morning provide the best viewing opportunities. During the early morning hours, birds tend to be active and vocal. Remember that other birds are nocturnal and begin their "day" at dusk, when they begin to feed on other night dwelling insects and animals.

- You are more likely to hear birds than to see them. Most birdcalls are male songbirds marking their territories or attempting to attract mates.

- Look for birds on the edges of habitats. The edges of rivers, streams, lakes, fields and forests are prime sites to locate and identify many different species of birds.

- Males are typically lavish in brilliant colors and are therefore often the more readily identifiable members of a given species.

Keeping these tips in mind will help to increase your chances of spotting a wide variety of birds. Armed with this guide and perhaps a trusty pair of binoculars, you should have good luck enjoying and identifying many of the birds common to the Missouri River valley. Don't forget to look up! Bluffs, treetops and bridge girders are great places to see nesting birds.

BIRD STUDY

P atience, persistence and practice go a long way to increasing your bird knowledge. However, as you begin to observe birds more closely, you will undoubtedly notice that there are common shapes, postures and flight patterns that, when combined with coloration and song, will help you to identify most birds correctly.

The following diagram will introduce you to some of the common features that are used by birders to identify different species.

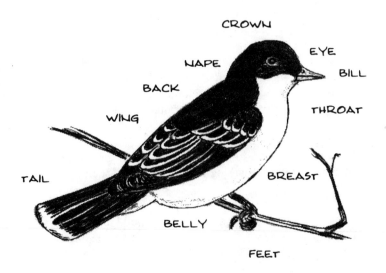

Questions to Aid Identification

Identifying birds is fun and easy to learn. Don't start by trying to memorize every bird species. Instead, just ask yourself a few questions when you see a bird that interests you:

- ✓ What size and shape is it?
- ✓ Is it a single color or several colors?
- ✓ What color is the breast? Is it different from the belly or the wings?
- ✓ Does the bird have stripes, spots or other definitive markings?
- ✓ What kind of tail does it have?
    Is it short, long, wide, narrow, flat, rounded or pointed?
- ✓ Does it have a crest?
- ✓ Is the beak thick and strong for seed opening?
    Or thin and sharp for insect eating?
- ✓ What kind of feet? Are they suited for walking, perching, climbing, swimming or holding prey?
- ✓ Where is it? On the ground or high in the canopy?
- ✓ Is it alone or with others?

A Sample Entry for Birds

COMMON NAME – SEASONAL STATUS (PR, SR, WR or T)
Scientific Name
Colors: Colors used for identification.
Size: Average size of adult, measured from tip of bill to tip of tail. When wing-spans are given, measurement indicates distance from wingtip to wintgtip.
Attracted to: Identifies common habitats. Also may include food preferences.
Song: Common vocal pattern or call, often used to identify the species.
Note: Often indicates local names or interesting habit or fact about the species.

Seasonal Status:

> **PR** —Permanent Resident
> **SR** —Summer Resident
> **WR** —Winter Resident
> **T** —Transient (migrates during spring or fall)

SMALL BIRDS
UP TO 7 INCHES

YELLOW

YELLOW WARBLER – T
Dendroica petechia
Colors: Yellow with olive green tinge on back. Male has reddish streaks on breast.
Size: From 4 to 5 in. long.
Attracted to: Riverside woodlands, wet thickets and brushy marsh edges.
Eats: Insects and spiders.
Song: "Sweet, sweet, sweet, I'm so sweet."

GOLDFINCH – PR
Carduelis tristis
Colors: Bright yellow with black head, wings and tail. White rump. Female is more gray and lacks black cap.
Size: From 4 to 5 in.
Attracted to: Fields, tree groves and thickets. Eats mostly seeds, especially thistle seeds. Also eats a few berries and tiny insects.
Song: Twitters, "swee." Flight call is "per-chik-o-ree."
Note: Often called the Wild Canary. Usually travels in flocks.

GREEN

RUBY-THROATED HUMMINGBIRD– SR
Archilochus colubris
Colors: Metallic green above, white below, ruby red throat and needle-like bill.
Size: Very small. No more than 3 1/2 in.
Attracted to: Gardens and woodlands. Likes red and orange flowers such as Bee Balm, Trumpet Vine and Jewelweed.
Song: "Tchew, tchew."
Note: This tiny bird can fly backward as well as forward, or hover in one spot or go straight up or down. It is constantly in motion and is the only "hummer" that visits Missouri.

BROWN

CEDAR WAXWING – T
Bombycilla cedrorum
Colors: Light beige to buff bird with crest. Black face pattern and yellow-tipped tail. Red spots on wings.
Size: From 5 to 7 in.
Attracted to: Wooded swamps, open forests and areas with scattered trees. Eats berries, flower petals and insects.
Song: A soft, high-pitched trill.
Note: They often pass a berry or flower petal back and forth until one bird finally eats it. Travel in flocks.

EASTERN PHOEBE – SR
Sayornis phoebe
Colors: Olive brown on top, dirty white belly. Black bill.
Size: From 5 to 7 in.
Attracted to: Banks of rivers and streams and along ledges of cliffs. Eats insects and spiders caught while in flight.
Song: "Fee-be, fee-be."
Note: One of the earliest arrivals in the spring and it returns to its same site year after year. Call is clearly "Phoe-be." Pumps or wags its tail.

BARN SWALLOW – SR
Hirundo rustica
Colors: Bluish-brown on top, throat is reddish-brown, buff or light red below, forked tail.
Size: From 5 to 6 1/2 in.
Attracted to: Insects and berries. Likes to nest under bridges and inside culverts. Can be in pairs or large colonies.
Song: A cheerful "sweeter-sweet, sweeter-sweet" twitter.

HOUSE SPARROW – PR
Passer domesticus
Colors: Brownish-gray with gray crown, black bib and bill.
Size: From 5 to 6 in.
Attracted to: Livestock farms and populated areas. An aggressive bird sometimes seen in flocks, these guys are everywhere.
Song: "Chissik, chissik."
Note: Also called the English Sparrow. Will drive songbirds such as Wrens, Bluebirds and Purple Martins from their nests and push out nestlings.

SONG SPARROW – WR
Melospiza melodia
Colors: Back and wings brown or brownish-gray and streaked. Breasts are white with dark streaks that often converge in a central spot. Tail may be rust colored.
Size: From 5 to 7 in.
Attracted to: Thickets and roadsides. Eats insects, seeds, grain and berries.
Song: Most common song is 3 or 4 short clear notes, a buzzy "towee," then a trill.
Note: Can sing as many as 20 different melodies and add variations to them.

HOUSE WREN – SR
Troglodytes aedon
Colors: Brown above and buff below. Chunky figure with a tail that points upward.
Size: From 3 1/2 to 4 3/4 in.
Attracted to: Brush, shrubs, orchards, farmyards and gardens.
Song: Often described as a cascade of sweet notes.
Note: A very inquisitive bird that will often respond to squeaky noises.

CAROLINA WREN – PR
Thryothorus ludovicianus
Colors: Rich brown back with black markings, white throat and buff-colored belly. White eye stripe.
Size: From 4 1/2 to 5 in.
Attracted to: Woodlands, hedgerows and undergrowth areas near water. Eats insects.
Song: Loud clear "teakettle, teakettle" or "cheery, cheery."

BLUE TO BLACK

PURPLE MARTIN – SR
Progne subis
Colors: Blue-black bird, forked tail and short bill. Female more gray, mottled throat and whitish belly.
Size: From 7 to 8 in.
Attracted to: Open areas usually near water. Eats flying insects and airborne spiders.
Song: Loud chirruping "too-too" and "too-too-weadle."
Note: Famous for the amount of insects they can eat in a day. The Native Americans hung gourd houses near their tipis to attract them.

INDIGO BUNTING – SR
Passerina cyanea
Colors: Brilliant deep blue that can look tur-quoise-blue in the sunlight or black in poor light. Female is drab brown.
Size: From 4 1/2 to 5 in.
Attracted to: Brushy areas, old pastures, wood-land clearings and the right-of-way of railroads where woodlands often meet open areas. They eat many insect pests and weed seeds.
Song: Series of high-pitched phrases, usually paired.

BLUEBIRD – SR (Sometimes WR)
Sialia sialis
Colors: Bright blue with orange-red throat and breast. Female is paler, almost gray.
Size: From 5 to 7 in.
Attracted to: Open areas, farmlands and especially fencerows. Eats spiders, insects and berries.
Song: "Chur chur-lee chur-lee."
Note: Missouri's state bird.

GRAY TO BLACK

BLUE-GRAY GNATCATCHER – SR
Polioptila caerulea
Colors: Blue-gray above and white below. Black tail is thin with white outer feathers.
Size: From 4 to 5 in.
Attracted to: Oak and mixed forests and groves along rivers.
Song: "Pwee, pwee, pwee." This is an ac-tive, fast-moving bird.

CHIMNEY SWIFT – SR
Chaetura pelagica
Colors: Dark gray-brown body, almost appearing black in flight.
Size: From 5 to 5 1/2 in. Small, cigar-shaped body with a short squared off tail. Long, narrow and swept-back wings.
Attracted to: They often nest in chimneys in towns, but also like the air shafts along the cliffs of the Missouri River and will swarm as they settle down for the night. They feed on flying insects and spiders that they catch mid-air.
Song: Loud chattering call.
Note: Birds rock from side to side with wings upraised. Their southern migration often marks the end of summer.

BLACK CAPPED CHICKADEE – PR
Parus atricapillus
Colors: Light gray with black cap and throat, white cheeks. Bellies are white and buff.
Size: Small bird. From 4 to 5 1/2 in.
Attracted to: Woodlands. Will winter over. Likes insects, seeds and berries.
Song: "Chick-a-dee-dee-dee."
Note: Usually travel in a group, often accompanied by other birds.

TUFTED TITMOUSE – PR
Parus bicolor
Colors: Crested gray bird with whitish belly. Black eyes and sharp beak.
Size: From 4 to 6 in.
Attracted to: Woodlands, wooded bottomlands and gardens. Likes insects and seeds, especially Sunflower seeds.
Song: "Peter, peter, peter."
Note: Can turn upside down to get insects from under leaves and twigs.

WHITE-BREASTED NUTHATCH – PR
Sitta carolinensis
Size: From 5 to 6 in.
Colors: Blue-gray with black crowns, white cheeks and bellies. Red-breasted nuthatches have rust-red underparts.
Attracted to: Deciduous forests for white-breasted birds. Coniferous forests for red-breasted birds. Eats seeds, nuts and small insects.
Song: Whistles and a nasal "yank."
Note: Short legs with unusually long toes and turned-down claws. Walks up or down a tree while foraging. Sometimes called the Upside-Down Bird.

DARK-EYED JUNCO – WR
Junco hyemalis
Colors: Gray or gray-brown with white belly, shows white along sides of tail. Pinkish bill. Can have black or gray head.
Size: From 5 to 6 in. Often mistaken for a sparrow.
Attracted to: Open woodlands and clearings. A ground feeder. Eats insects, seeds and berries.
Song: Musical trill on one pitch. Sometimes rapid twittering.
Note: Also called the Snowbird. Often found in small flocks.

DOWNY WOODPECKER – PR
Picoides pubescens
Colors: Black and white with white belly. Red nape patch. Short thick bill.
Size: Smallest of the woodpeckers, only 5–7 in.
Attracted to: Open woodlands and orchards. Eats wood-boring insects, berries and seeds.
Song: "Pik" and soft whinny.

MEDIUM BIRDS FROM 7 TO 12 INCHES

ORANGE TO RED

CARDINAL – PR
Cardinalis cardinalis
Colors: Bright red body and prominent crest with black around eyes and conical bill. Female is brown with buff-colored breast and red on wings and tail.
Size: From 7 to 8 1/2 in.
Attracted to: Brushy woodlands, thickets and shrubbery. Eats seeds, berries and insects.
Song: "Purty, purty, purty."
Note: These birds mate for life.

ROBIN – SR
Turdus migratorius
Colors: Bright red-orange breast, black head with white around eye. Back is grayish-brown. Bill is yellow.
Size: From 8 to 11 in.
Attracted to: Open woods, forest borders and farmland. Eats earthworms, insects and berries.
Song: "Cheerily cheerio" or "tut, tut, tut."
Note: One of the first returning birds of spring. Found nearly everywhere.

NORTHERN ORIOLE – SR
Icterus galbula
Colors: Bright orange with black head, wings and tail.
Size: From 6 to 8 1/2 in.
Attracted to: Shade trees and open woodlands. Eats insects and fruit.
Song: "Hewli, hewli, hewli."
Note: Nest is a suspended pouch that is built high up in leafy trees. Nest is often only visible after leaves have fallen off the tree.

BLUE

BLUE JAY – PR
Cyanocitta cristata
Colors: Bright blue above including distinctive crest, white spots and black bars on wings and tail. Black necklace.
Size: From 9 to 12 in.
Attracted to: Both deciduous and coniferous forests, but likes oak

trees best. Eats nuts, seeds, fruits and insects.
Song: "Jay, jay, jay" is the best known of its many calls.
Note: Can sometimes be a bully, but also loudly warns of approaching predators.

BROWN

KILLDEER – T
Charadrius vociferus
Colors: Brown with two black bars across white throat and breast, reddish rump and tail.
Size: From 8 1/2 to 11 in.
Attracted to: Prairies, meadows, gravel bars and mudflats.
Song: "Kill-dee" or "dee-dee-dee."
Note: Will lead you away from their nest by presenting a broken wing act.

BROWN THRASHER – SR
Toxostoma rufum
Colors: Red-brown above, two white wing bars, white with brown streaks below. Yellow eye.
Size: From 10 1/2 to 12 in.
Attracted to: Brush, woodland edges and hedgerows.
Song: Sings loudly and has many different songs. Some sound like "chuck," or "churr," usually repeated 2 or 3 times.

EASTERN MEADOWLARK – PR
Sturnelia magna
Colors: Dark brown-gray on top with dusky gray edges. Yellow underside with black V-shaped breast band. White edges.
Size: From 9 1/2 to 10 in.
Attracted to: Open areas, prairies and meadows.
Song: "See-you, see-yeer."

NORTHERN BOB WHITE – PR
Colinus virginianus
Colors: Reddish-brown with white throat and white streaks on sides. Male has black and white stripes on face. Female is brown and buff.
Size: From 8 to 10 in.
Attracted to: Underbrush in meadows and pastures. Sometimes in open woodlands. Feeds on seeds, insects, berries and leaves.
Song: "Bob-white."
Note: Usually travels in coveys or groups of 12–15.

HORNED LARK – PR
Eremophila alpestris
Colors: Streaked brown back, white outer tail feathers. Black "horns" on head and broad black stripe under eyes. Breast is yellow to cream with black V-shaped bib.
Size: From 6 1/2 to 8 in.
Attracted to: Prairies and other open areas. Eats insects, grain, seeds and spiders.
Song: "Tsee-eee or tsee-titi."

Note: Because their nests are often in hay fields, many are destroyed by mowers.

Gray & Black

EASTERN KINGBIRD – SR
Tyrannus tyrannus
Colors: Gray back and black head. Underside is white with light gray on breast, tail has white band at the tip.
Size: From 7 1/2 to 8 1/2 in.
Attracted to: Woodland clearings and farms near water.
Song: Hard "dzeet, dzeet, dzeet."
Note: This bird will aggressively defend its territory. Known to attack passing crows or hawks by swooping down on the intruder and pulling or plucking out its feathers—may even land on the intruder in an attempt to knock it out of the sky.

NORTHERN MOCKINGBIRD – PR
Mimus polyglotto
Colors: Gray above and lighter gray below. Two wing bars on each wing and white feathers under the wings. Tail is black with white border.
Size: From 9 to 11 in.
Attracted to: Open woods and populated areas. Likes insects, spiders and fruit.
Song: "Check, check, check."
Note: Can imitate more than 30 different birdcalls and songs.

STARLING – PR
Sturnus vulgaris
Color: Black with green and purple gloss. Long pointed yellow bill, short square tail and chunky body.
Size: From 7 to 8 in.
Attracted to: Farmlands, brushy areas and often a pest in towns. Eats destructive insects.
Song: Squeaks, twitters and imitates the calls of other birds.
Note: They gather in large bunches. Considered a crop pest during their fall migration. Introduced to New York 100 years ago from Europe, they are now found almost everywhere and compete with native species.

ROCK DOVE OR PIGEON – PR
Columba livia
Colors: Chunky body wit a lot of variations in color. Often gray with white rump, 2 black bars across wings and dark tail tip.
Size: From 10 to 11 in. Chunky.
Attracted to: Towns and farms along the river. Also in cliffs and along high rock ledges. Eat seeds, grain and scraps from humans.
Song: Soft "coo-cuk-cuk-cuk-coo."
Note: One of America's most familiar birds.

MOURNING DOVE – SR
Zenaida macroura
Colors: Soft beige-gray with long, pointed tail, ending with a tip of white feathers.
Size: From 10 to 12 in. Slender and small headed.
Attracted to: Dense shrubs and open areas. Eats seeds and insects.
Song: "Oh-woo, woo, woo, woo."
Note: The most abundant and widespread of all the doves.

ROSE-BREASTED GROSBEAK – T
Pheucticus ludovicianus
Colors: Black and white bird with rose-colored breast patch and fat white bill.
Size: From 7 to 8 in.
Attracted to: Woodlands and shrubby areas near streams.
Song: Melodious and robin-like. Call is a sharp "eek."
Note: Appear in April or early May.

COWBIRD – SR
Molothrus ater
Color: Glossy black with dark brown head. Female is gray-brown above and paler below.
Size: From 6 to 8 in.
Attracted to: Farmlands, river woodlands, edges of forests and towns.
Song: Sort of a rattle with squeaks.
Note: A troublesome bird that is causing a decline of many native species. Known to lay its eggs in the nests of others. Its precocious young frequently out eat and starve nest mates.

RED-WINGED BLACKBIRD – SR
Agelaius phoeniceus
Colors: Glossy black with red shoulders. Female is dark brown and heavily streaked.
Size: From 7 to 9 in.
Attracted to: Grasslands and marshes. Eats seeds, grains, insects and spiders.
Song: "Tonk-a-leee, tonk-a-leee" with a trill at the end.
Note: An early spring returner, this very common bird is found in huge flocks during winter.

RED-BELLIED WOODPECKER – PR
Melanerpes carolinus
Colors: Barred black and white above, buff-gray below. Red crown.
Size: From 8 to 8 1/2 in.
Attracted to: Open woodlands, farmlands and orchards. Eats insects, fruit and seeds.
Song: "Churr" or "chiv, chiv."

RED-HEADED WOODPECKER – SR
Melanerpes erthrocephalus
Colors: Black above, white underneath and on wings. Red head.
Size: From 7 to 8 in.
Attracted to: Groves, open woodlands, farmlands and shade trees. Likes to nest in large limbs of dead trees. Eats wood-boring insects and nuts, but will also eat spiders, earthworms, birds' eggs, mice, nuts, tree bark, berries and corn.
Song: Sharp "queark."
Note: Habitat loss and competition with Starlings for nest holes have greatly reduced their numbers.

COMMON GRACKLE – SR
Quiscalus quiscula
Colors: Glossy black with iridescent purple, green and bronze. Yellow eyes, long keel-shaped tail and stout bill.
Size: From 10 to 12 in.
Attracted to: Open fields and tree groves. Eats insects, seeds, grain, eggs and young of other birds, sometimes small fish.
Song: Harsh, guttural and squeaking noises. Call is often a "chack."
Note: Sounds like a rusty hinge.

Large Birds
from 12 to 45 inches
Blue to Green to Gray

KINGFISHER – PR
Ceryle alcyon
Colors: Blue-gray back, white breast with a blue-gray band near throat. Female has a second rusty band across belly. Dagger-shaped bill and ragged crest.
Size: From 12 to 14 in.
Attracted to: Tree-lined rivers and lakes. Seldom seen far from water. Dives from the air to catch fish. Also eats crabs, crayfish and mice.
Song: Loud, dry rattle.
Note: Nests in steep banks burrows as deep as 15 ft.

BLUE-WINGED TEAL – T
Anas discors
Color: Head brownish-gray, neck white. Male has white crescents below its eyes. Body is mostly gray with light blue shoulder patches. Female is mottled brown with blue patch on wings.
Size: From 14 to 16 in.
Attracted to: Ponds, marshes and other shallow-water areas. Eats seeds, snails, insects and aquatic plants.

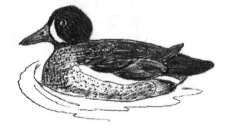

Song: Males whistle and females deliver a high-pitched quack.
Note: Expect to see these small ducks migrating south in September and north in late March most often with other species.

GIANT CANADA GOOSE – PR
Branta canadensis
Colors: Black head and neck with white cheek patch. Body is gray brown. Undertail feathers are white.
Size: From 25 to 44 in. Wingspan up to 5 ft.
Attracted to: Rivers, freshwater marshes and fields of grain. Likes to eat aquatic plants, grass, grain and small aquatic animals. Nests in cliffs.
Song: Honking, especially in flight.
Note: Famous for its V-formations in flight, often flying up to 45 miles per hour. On the ground if sensing danger, a bird can flatten itself out to resemble a rock. Present all year. Long thought to be extinct.

GREAT BLUE HERON – SR
(WR when water stays open)
Ardea herodias
Colors: Gray-blue with white head and two black crown stripes. Yellow bill.
Size: Up to 48 in.
Attracted to: Rivers and shorelines. Nests in large rookeries, but is a solitary feeder. Hunts fish, snakes, frogs and small mammals.
Song: Guttural squawks—similar to harsh goose call.

GREEN HERON – SR
Butorides striatus
Color: Dark green-gray, head and neck chestnut, crown black with a crest. Dull yellow legs except during breeding, then can be bright orange.
Size: Crow size, 14–22 in.
Attracted to: Rivers, streams, mudflats and other moist areas. Feeds on fish, frogs, crayfish and insects. Nests in isolated pairs or in small groups.
Song: Loud "kwick."
Note: Also known as the Green-Backed Heron.

KESTREL – PR
Falco sparverius
Colors: Reddish back, blue-gray wings and black bar at tip of tail. Double black stripes on white face.
Size: From 9 to 12 in.
Attracted to: Open wooded areas, prairies and farmlands. Often seen in treetops, tops of poles or flying above farm fields. Eats insects, small mammals and other birds.
Song: "Killy, killy, killy."
Note: Formerly called Sparrow Hawk. This is the smallest and most common falcon.

BROWN

NORTHERN FLICKER – PR
Colaptes auratus

Colors: A large brown woodpecker with a black breast band and mustache, white rump and yellow wing linings.

Size: From 10 to 11 in.

Attracted to: Woodlands or open country with trees. Most important food is ants, but also eats insects, fallen fruits and seeds.

Song: "Wick-er, wick-er, wick-er" or "wic, wic, wic, wic."

Note: Its tongue can extend nearly 3 inches, making it easy for it to catch ants. Usually feeds on the ground. Distinguished by undulating flight pattern.

RED-TAILED HAWK – PR
Buteo jamaicensis

Colors: A stocky dark brown bird with white breast and rust-colored tail.

Size: From 19 to 25 in. Wingspan 4 1/2 ft.

Attracted to: Farmlands and open woodlands. Eats rodents and other small mammals, but also small birds and large insects. Can often be seen sitting on fenceposts.

Song: Loud, descending "keeeer."

Note: Members of this species, like many other birds of prey, tend to circle high above in the sky riding rising streams of hot air (called thermals). They are usually seen with their wings fully extended and can stay up with little flapping or effort.

WILD TURKEY – PR
Meleagris gallopavo
Colors: Bronze with black barring, bluish head and neck with no feathers and red wattle. Fan-shaped tail tipped with a red-brown color. Female is lighter colored and lacks beard. Thinner than domestic turkeys.
Size: From 36 to 48 in.
Attracted to: Woodland clearings and brushy forest edges. Likes to eat seeds, nuts, berries and insects. Usually forages in small flocks.
Song: A gobbling call.
Note: They roost in trees and are fast on their feet! At one time almost became extinct due to unregulated hunting.

BARRED OWL – PR
Strix varia
Colors: Brown with darker brown barring on upper breast, darker brown streaking below. Large dark eyes.
Size: From 17 to 24 in. Can have a wingspan of up to 4 ft.
Attracted to: Small mammals, birds and insects. Likes deep woods, especially near water.
Song: "Who cooks for you? Who cooks for you all?"

BALD EAGLE – T

Haliaeetus leucocephalus

Colors: Dark brown with thick yellow beak. Adult has white head and tail, usually some amounts of white feathers on its body.

Size: From 35 to 40 in. Can have a wingspan of up to 8 ft.

Attracted to: Rivers and lakes. Nest looks like a heap of sticks usually in a tall tree and near water, getting quite large as the eagle keeps adding to it from year to year. Hunts fish, small mammals and waterbirds that they capture on the run and carrion, especially dead fish on the shores of rivers, streams and lakes.

Song: Loud cackles.

Note: Our national emblem.

The Missouri River valley is a popular winter retreat for bald eagles. The abundant food and cover in the region make a perfect winter habitat for eagles who are flying south to their summer breeding grounds. These magnificent birds add much beauty and splendor to the river valley.

- The state of Missouri has one of the largest winter bald eagle populations.

- An eagle's eyesight is 5 or 6 times sharper than a human's.

- In the wild, an eagle may live to be greater than 30 years of age.

- The majority of an eagle's diet consists of fish, while a minor part includes dead or injured birds or mammals.

- They are known to exceed flight speeds over 100 miles per hour during a dive. Normal flight speeds range from 20 to 40 miles per hour.

- Immature bald eagles (less than 5 years old) are entirely brown. Mature eagles have white heads and tails, beaks and eyes are yellow, body feathers are black.

BLACK

PILEATED WOODPECKER – PR
Dryocopus pileatus
Colors: Mainly black with a prominent red crest. White stripes down neck and across face. Male has red mustache. Wings have white linings. Bill is black.
Size: From 15 to 19 in.
Attracted to: Mature forests with large trees. Eats ants and other wood-boring insects, sometimes berries.
Song: Loud "wuck-a-wuck-a-wuck-a."
Note: To see one requires careful stalking.

AMERICAN CROW – PR
Corvus brachyrhynchos
Colors: All black bird with fan-shaped tail.
Size: From 17 to 21 in.
Attracted to: Farmlands, woodlands and open spaces. Eats almost anything. Fond of corn, but will eat insects such as grasshoppers and cutworms. Also eats small reptiles, eggs, small birds and carrion.
Song: "Caw, caw, caw."
Note: This is an intelligent and mischievous bird, sometimes given to stealing bright-colored objects.

TURKEY VULTURE – SR
Cathartes aura
Colors: Black with grey feathers underneath the wings. No feathers on head, which is red.
Size: From 26 to 32 in. Can have a wingspan of up to 6 ft.
Attracted to: A true scavenger. Prefers flesh of dead animals. Will hunt small mammals and birds. Likes open countryside, farmland and forests.
Song: A hiss.
Note: Can be confused with the black vulture, which is smaller, more stocky and given to flapping. Generally not in this area. Flies in a shallow V and does more gliding than flapping. Often called a buzzard.

Aᴛᴇʀ ᴛʜᴇ Fʟᴏᴏᴅ ᴏꜰ 1993

The following species have been spotted
more frequently since the flood of 1993.

Wʜɪᴛᴇ

GREAT EGRET – T
Casmerodius albus
Size: From 36 to 40 in.
Colors: White with black legs and feet. Yellow bill that appears orange during the breeding season (lacks hook but has a black tip).
Attracted to: Wetlands, marshes, ponds, mud flats and shorelines. Primarily eats small fish and crayfish.
Song: Low, rough croaks. Sometimes bark, "cuk, cuk, cuk."

WHITE PELICAN – T
Pelecanus erythrorhychos
Colors: White with black wing tips. Large, bright yellowish-orange bill. (Immature will have darker, dusky bill.)
Size: From 54 to 70 in. Can have a wingspan of up to 9 1/2 ft.
Attracted to: Lakes, rivers and marshes. Primarily eat fish scooped from the water while swimming.
Song: Low, gutteral groan.
Note: Typically fly in organized single-file lines or V-shaped patterns.

Bʟᴀᴄᴋ

DOUBLE-CRESTED CORMORANT – T
Phalacrocorax auritus
Colors: Black. Often have pale orange marking on face. Slender, yellowish bill with a hooked tip.
Size: From 30 to 36 in.
Attracted to: Lakes and rivers. Eats fish and crustaceans.
Song: Mostly silent. May give grunt-like call when nesting in large numbers.
Note: Often perches on rocks or posts and may stand with both wings spread out. When standing erect, neck often has S-shaped appearance.

Ducks

MALLARD – PR

Anas platyrhynchos

Colors: Green head with a white neck ring, yellow bill, chestnut breast, purplish-blue wing patch bordered with 2 white stripes. Female is mottled brown with purple-blue wing patches and a white tail.

Size: From 16 to 28 in.

Attracted to: Swamps, marshes and other wet areas. Eats seeds, snails, insects and small fish.

Song: Female's call is a loud "quack."

WOOD DUCK – T

Aix sponsa

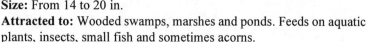

Colors: Crested with white throat and chestnut breast. Body iridescent blues, greens and purples. Red bill and buff flanks. Female is mottled gray-brown with white eye patches.

Size: From 14 to 20 in.

Attracted to: Wooded swamps, marshes and ponds. Feeds on aquatic plants, insects, small fish and sometimes acorns.

Song: "Ooo-eek."

Note: They usually travel in pairs and mate for life. Best observed in early morning hours.

Wɑɴᴛ ᴛᴏ Kɴᴏᴡ Mᴏʀᴇ?
Bʀɪɴɢ ɑʟᴏɴɢ ɑɴ Exᴘᴇʀɪᴇɴᴄᴇᴅ Bɪʀᴅᴇʀ Cᴏᴍᴘɑɴɪᴏɴ:

One of the best ways to increase your knowledge of birds, their songs, behavior and habitats is to bring a more experienced birder along on your trip. Here are some organizations that support bird-study activities and have regular outings:

Burroughs Audubon Society of Kansas City
Rt. 3 Box 120
Blue Springs, MO 64015

Columbia Audubon Society
P.O. Box 1331
Columbia, MO 65205

National Audubon Society
200 Southwind Place
Manhattan, KS 66502

Webster Groves Nature Study Society
P.O. Box 190065
St. Louis, MO 63119

Audubon Society of Missouri's Hotline
(information and bird sightings): (573) 445-9115

BUTTERFLIES

Butterflies are beautiful to watch and important plant pollinators. Their presence indicates a healthy ecosystem. They do not sting, bite or transmit disease. A butterfly is a daytime insect with 6 jointed legs, 3 body segments, 2 antennae and 2 pairs of wings. The tips of the antennae are used for smelling and touching. The wings are covered with colorful scales.

Their primary food source is nectar from plants, which they extract through a coiled, tongue-like proboscis made up of 2 linked tubes that work like straws. In flight, the proboscis is coiled up tightly against the face of the butterfly, but can quickly be fully extended to drink nectar or other liquids.

Butterfly colors are the result of thousands of tiny, shingle-like scales attached to a thin, fragile wing membrane. Red, orange, yellow and brown come from the actual color of each scale. Iridescent colors such as blue, green, violet, silver and gold are the result of tiny structures on the scale surface that bend and reflect light. It is better to study butterflies without catching them, since handling them can damage their delicate wings.

The four states of metamorphosis are: ova (egg), larva (caterpillar), pupa or chrysalis (cocoon) and adult butterfly. It is interesting to note that growth only occurs during the larva stage. In other words, growth does not occur in the adult butterfly—so little butterflies don't grow into large butterflies.

Common Butterfly Families

SKIPPERS

Identified by a swift, bouncing and erratic flight. The erratic flight helps them evade hungry birds. They have fat little bodies, relatively small wings and distinctive hooks at the ends of their antennae. These are very small butterflies.

Size: Around 1 in., but can range up to 2 1/2 in.

Colors: Brown, orange or black and usually drab.

Attracted to: Brushy fields and roadsides, both black and honey locust, wisteria and other flowers. Can be seen close-up along roadsides and in meadows.

Season: Early April through mid-October.

Note: Skippers are members of the family *Hesperiidae*, a large family containing several thousand species.

SWALLOWTAILS

Identified by their well-developed wing appendage or tail, that extends from the rear of each hind wing.

Size: From 2 to 4 in.

Colors: Generally black with orange or yellow markings.

Attracted to: Mud puddles, damp soil, open fields and meadows.

Season: Late March through October.

Note: Members of the large family *Papilionidae*, which includes over 700 different species.

BRUSH-FOOTED BUTTERFLIES
Identified by short hairy front legs and big bodies.
Size: From 2 to 3 in.
Colors: Generally tones of orange or brown with yellow and black markings.
Attracted to: Marshes and other damp areas including mud puddles, fresh animal waste and rotting fruit.
Season: Mid-May through early October.
Note: Members of the largest family, *Nymphalidae*, which contains several thousand species.

SULPHURS & WHITES
Identified by their small size, active flight patterns and distinctive coloration.
Size: A relatively small butterfly, between 1 and 1 1/2 in.
Colors: Usually yellow, orange or white, often with black borders or markings on their wings. The all-yellow color of the common European sulphur was the origin of the word butterfly. The primarily white butterfly is known as the Cabbage Butterfly and is considered a pest. It is also one of the first butterflies to emerge in the spring.
Attracted to: Cabbage and related plants, also clover. Found in open fields and yards.
Season: March through December.
Note: Members of the large family *Pieridae*, which includes nearly 2,000 species.

BLUES &
COMMON BROWN HAIRSTREAK

Identified by hairlike tails on the hind wings and the narrow bands of color on the underside. Both Browns and Blues have a swift darting flight pattern. These butterflies hold their wings folded over their back when resting.

Size: Generally 1 in. or less.

Colors: Blues are usually blue and blue-gray, sometimes with orange markings on the underside of their wings. The Common Brown Hairstreak is brown, sometimes with orange and black markings.

Attracted to: Roadsides, fields and other open areas. Likes flowers.

Season: Generally April through October—some exceptions.

Note: Member of the family *Lycaenidae*, which includes several thousand varieties, including the smallest butterfly in North America.

MONARCH BUTTERFLIES

Identified by bold orange and black markings. Also called the Milkweed Butterfly. In the fall, as they migrate southward, one can see them cover entire trees as they rest.

Size: Generally 3 1/2–4 in. One of the largest butterflies.

Colors: Striking orange and black. Males have a dark spot in the middle of each hind wing that gives off a scent to attract females.

Attracted to: Milkweed, Dogbane and related plants.

Season: Usually found in June through August, sometimes early September. Begin migration in late summer.

Note: These summertime residents are members of the family *Danaidae*, which includes fewer than 300 species.

Weighing less than half a gram, many **monarch** butterflies migrate 2,000 miles to their winter quarters. A small alpine forest 75 miles west of Mexico City, Mexico, is home to more than 100 million of these beautiful butterflies each winter. Each year, the new monarch population is about 5 generations removed from the ones that made the trip the previous year. No one knows how each new generation finds this wintering spot since none have ever been there before.

INSECTS

CHIGGERS

A chigger is a type of mite, not an insect. Eggs are laid on low vegetation, and the larvae, on hatching, attach to a passing host. Chiggers are so small they're hard to see and are seldom noticed until their bite begins to cause irritation and itching. On people they like to attach themselves to the areas where clothing is tightest. Dusting oneself at the ankles and wrists with a combination of powdered sulfur (which smells like rotten eggs) and nice-smelling talcum powder is a good deterrent. They are most active in the early summer months.

MIDGES

You don't have to look for midges, they'll find you. They look like tiny mosquitoes, but their wings are transparent. They do not bite, but they do **SWARM**—in fact, the humming of such a swarm may be audible a long way off. Midges are most active near the water and in the evening. They like decaying matter and moist ground and are an important food for fish.

NO-SEE-UMS

These are very small biting midges—their bite is out of proportion to their size. They do not travel far from where they were born and you can often escape them by simply moving a few yards away. The larvae can be found in sand, mud, even the water in tree holes. Sometimes called Punkies.

TICKS

This tiny bug is not an insect. Like a spider, it has 4 pairs of legs. Ticks in Missouri are almost always the Lone Star Tick or the American Dog Tick. They are found in low bushy areas and are parasitic—attacking animals, birds, reptiles, also humans if the opportunity presents itself. A leg brushed against low vegetation may find itself the main meal for as many as 200 seed ticks! When you come in from a walk in the woods or across the fields, check your body carefully. Ticks can transmit serious diseases, but this is not a very common occurrence.

Spiders

These interesting little insect relatives have 8 legs rather than 6, and 2 rather than 3 body sections. Spiders are not insects, they are arachnids. There are many different kinds of spiders, of the more than 300 species of spiders in Missouri only two are dangerous: the Brown Recluse and the Black Widow.

Many young spiders and even some mature males travel great distances by riding the wind. They achieve flight by releasing a liquid protein from their abdomens that, once exposed to the air, turns into a solid silk-like thread. These long threads, called Gossamers, catch the prevailing winds and carry the spiders into the air. This type of air travel allows spiders to travel to new places and lessens crowding. Be sure to watch for these flying arachnids!

Jumping spiders
Often brightly colored or iridescent
and can be found under stones and in debris.

Wolf spiders
Also called Ground Spiders. Most are dark brown and are recognized by their eyes. There are 4 small eyes in the first row, 2 large eyes in the second row and 2 small or medium-size eyes in the third row. When the young hatch, they are carried around on the back of the female for a time.

Missouri's Two Poisonous Spiders

Brown Recluse

(Loxosceles reclusa)
With a violin-like marking on its back, the Brown Recluse is usually found in homes, has a serious bite, but is rarely fatal. This spider can be found in the outdoors in secluded well-sheltered locations littered with loose debris.

Black Widow

(Latrodectus mactans)
Female has a reddish-orange hourglass-shaped spot on the stomach. Males have 4 pairs of reddish-orange stripes along the sides of the stomach. This is the most poisonous spider in Missouri. It can be—but usually is not—fatal. They can be found on and under stumps and fallen branches, or in holes in the ground.

Velvet Mites

From the size of a pinhead to 1/8 in. Easily recognized by their bright red coloring, they are known as red bugs. Parasites on insects, spiders and Daddy Longlegs. Often crawling on limestone and other rock faces.

Daddy Longlegs

From 1/8 to 1/4 in. body with 8 extremely long stilt-like legs. The head is not separated from the body. You can find them almost everywhere. Treat them kindly. They are fragile. Count the legs on the Daddy Longlegs you see. Many are missing legs and carry bright Velvet Mites on their backs.

Mosquitoes

Can grow to 1/2 in., sometimes larger. Usually brown or brown-gray. Have long legs, a single pair of wings and a stiletto-like mouth part. Only the females buzz and bite. They are usually found near still water. They are most active during the twilight hours, at night or in dense shade.

Ants

Ants are everywhere and can be from 1/10 to 1/4 in. There are many types of ants, from red to dark brown and black. Their abdomen is joined to the thorax by a thin midsection. They have a big bottom and bent antennae. Ants live in colonies and are fascinating to watch, as they are very well organized and communal.

Horseflies

These are from 1/4 to 1 in., and you need not worry about finding one. A horsefly considers you one of its favorite meals. They have a big head, their eyes are often iridescent, bodies are patterned light and dark and they make an unmistakable buzzing sound.

Grasshoppers

These are from 1/2 to 2 in., gray or gray-brown, sometimes with brightly colored hind wings and can be found during the summer months in grasslands and fields all over Missouri. Katydids are much the same, except they are usually green, with broad, long antennae and are found in woods and bushy areas as well as fields.

Wasps

There are a great variety of these creatures. From 1/4 to 1 in. These insects have black shiny bodies, sometimes with yellow markings. Their wings fold parallel to their body at rest. Mud Daubers are the ones that build the mud nests in barns, under eaves and so on.

Honey Bees

These bees are tan and slender with some black. From 1/2 to 1 1/4 in. They are important pollinators of flowers. They live in hollow trees or man-made hives, but can usually be found buzzing from flower to flower.

Bumble Bees

Larger, even more hairs, yellow and black.

Sweat Bees

Technically not a bee but a wasp. Small, brilliantly colored and attracted to perspiration.

Cicadas

From 1/2 to 2 in. These broad-headed insects have transparent or semi-transparent wings. Can be found in woods and brushy areas. Their steady hum often fills the summer evening air during August. Look for their shedded hulls stuck to tree bark in the summer time.

Walking Sticks

Up to 6 in., this insect is slow moving. You'll have to look closely because they do look like a twig. Legs are very long and slim. No wings. Long antennae. Found in woods, on trees or shrubs.

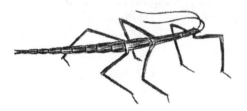

Dragonflies

Slender insects from 1 1/2 to 4 in., usually black or brown, often with bright marking. The wings are transparent and held straight out when the body is at rest. They live on or near water.

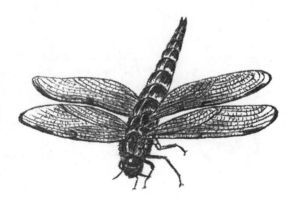

Damselflies

From 1 to 3 in. with needle-like irides-cent bodies. Wings are transparent, folded or open and slightly uplifted at rest. They live on or near water.

Water Striders

This thin bug from 1/2 to 3/4 in., has front legs shorter than its hind legs. Skates rapidly on surface film in slow-moving water.

Whirligig Beetles

A black or dark green oval beetle from 1/8 to 3/4 in., with long front legs, found on water where it swims in circles on the surface. Its eyes are in 2 parts, which means it can look up and down at the same time.

Ladybugs

This is one of our most valued beetles because they feed on aphids and are often used to control pests. All have very short legs. They are red-orange, but the number of black spots on their backs can range from 2 to 15. In win-ter, they hibernate under fallen branches and rocks.

Ground Beetles

One of the most common and abundant of beetles. Can be found on the ground beneath objects, sometimes on vegetation or flowers. They often run rapidly when dis-turbed. One species of ground beetle gives off an un-pleasant odor when handled. It is nicknamed the Stink-bug. The secretion is foul and irritating to skin.

Mammals

Many different mammals are common in the Missouri River valley. They are warm-blooded, air-breathing vertebrates and three main characteristics define this diverse group: (1) all females have mammary glands (they produce milk); (2) all mammals have hair at least at some stage in their lives; and (3) with the exception of two species that are not found in North America, all mammals are born alive and nourish their young inside their body cavities.

Although abundant, many mammals are difficult to spot and identify because they are secretive, wary of human encounters and are often most active at night or twilight. Commonly only the smaller species such as rabbits, squirrels and mice will be seen by the casual observer. Despite these obstacles, visitors to the region are often surprised by the number of mammals that they are able to observe.

To study the wide range of mammals as they occur in the Missouri River valley, it is helpful to keep the following tips in mind:

● Pass cautiously and quietly through mammal habitats. Avoid sudden movements and loud noises. If you make a loud noise, freeze immediately—you will have a better chance of keeping the wildlife near if you remain still.

● Don't let your clothes or equipment give you away. Avoid bright colors and loud fabrics and make sure that your camera and binoculars do not rattle or reflect brightly. Avoid wearing strong scents such as heavily perfumed soaps, deodorants and colognes. Many mammals have a keen sense of smell and your scent will give you away.

Mammals

● Travel in the shadows. Most mammals can easily detect individuals with sun on their backs or when they are silhouetted against the sky.

● In addition to looking for the actual animal, learn to recognize tracks, paths, droppings and to identify their dens, nest or burrows. Proper identification of these clues will go a long way toward helping you identify the wildlife that is common to the area. Remember that learning to read tracks and other indirect signs is a skill that develops slowly over years of observing nature.

● Moist soil around water, along trails or following periods of light snow offer the best opportunities for studying tracks. You may often find the footprints of egrets, deer and raccoons all mixed together near watering holes.

● If you are exploring after dark, you may notice eyes reflecting back at you. You can still identify many animals by the distinctive colors that reflect back at you:

Identify Mammals at Night by the Color Reflected from their Eyes:

White = Deer
Bright white = Coyote or Fox
Dull yellow = Bobcat
Bright yellow = Raccoon
Dull orange = Opossum
Amber = Skunk
Pink = Squirrel

A Sample Entry for Mammals

COMMON NAME
Scientific Name
Size: Size of average adult measured from tip of nose to base of tail. Tail measurements give length from base to tip (does not include fur extending past the fleshy tip of tail).
Description: Body type, color, identifying features or marks.
Where to find: Most common habitats.
Note: May include other local names, interesting facts or trivia.

SHREW
Blarina brevicauda
Size: From 1 to 2 1/2 in.
Description: Gray-brown fur. Almost no ears. Elongated body. Pointed nose. Very small eyes.
Where to find: Grasslands, bushy areas and forests.
Note: Will eat their weight every day. This is the smallest mammal in Missouri.

DEER MOUSE
Peromyscus maniculatus
Size: From 3 to 4 in.
Tail, 2–5 in.
Description: Brownish-gray. White feet and belly. Tail is white below and dark above.
Where to find: Nearly everywhere.

MOLE
Scalopus aquaticus
Size: From 4 to 6 in.
Description: Long pink snout. Eyes are small. Has huge front feet and stubby tail. Fur is very soft and gray to dark brown.
Where to find: Lives in moist grassy areas and looser soil about 10 in. underground.

Note: This is the creature that creates those long raised burrows that drive gardeners crazy. Although sometimes a nuisance, these burrows help aerate the soil.

CHIPMUNK
Tamias striatus
Size: From 5 to 6 in.
Tail, 3–4 in.
Description: Reddish-brown fur. Black stripes on head, sides and back.
Where to find: Brushy areas and forests.
Note: A ground-dwelling squirrel. Lives in burrows.

RAT
Rattus norvegicus
Size: From 7 to 10 in.
Tail, 5–8 in.
Description: Fur is dull gray brown and whitish underneath. Long scaly, almost hairless tail.
Where to find: Dumps and fields.
Note: Eats almost anything, dead or alive.

MUSKRAT
Ondatra zibethicus
Size: From 9 to 15 in.
Tail, 7–11 in.
Description: Reddish-brown, light gray belly and black scaly tail.
Where to find: Near water ledges.
Note: Builds water lodges like Beaver, but with grasses and sedges instead of sticks and mud.

BAT
Myotis—several species
Size: From 3 to 4 in. Wingspan, 8–10 in.
Description: Dark and shiny fur. Low zig-zag flight. Usually emerges just at twilight.
Where to find: Wooded areas near water and in caves.
Note: They fly like birds, but bats are mammals. Do not pick a bat up. Sick or injured bats can transmit rabies. During summer nights, a great variety of bats can be seen in the air—17 species frequent Missouri. Also, some bat species such as the Gray Bat are endangered and their habitats are often protected during certain times of the year—they should not be disturbed.

GRAY SQUIRREL
Sciurus carolinensis
Size: From 8 to 11 in. Tail, 8–10 in.
Description: Gray fur above and grayish-white below. Large bushy tail.
Where to find: Broadleaf forests.
Note: Gray squirrels are noisy. "Kuk, kuk, kuk" means danger. Rapid jerks of its tail means it is threatened. Rapid waves of its tail are a sign of agitation. Tail against the back means the danger has passed.

FOX SQUIRREL
Sciurus niger
Size: From 10 to 15 in. Tail, 9–14 in.
Description: Rusty fur above and whitish below. Bushy tail.
Where to find: In trees and forested areas.
Note: Especially active immediately after sunrise and just before sunset.

WEASEL
Mustela frenata
Size: From 7 to 15 in.
Tail, 3–7 in.
Description: Long, slim body.
Tail black at tip, brown body fur.
Yellowish-white underneath.
Where to find: Open country,
forests and often near water.

MINK
Mustela vison
Size: From 11 to 20 in.
Tail, 5–9 in.
Description: Long,
slim body. Dark red-
brown, white spots on
belly and chin.
Where to find: Along
waterways.

OPOSSUM
Didelphis virginiana
Size: From 13 to 21 in.
Tail, 9–20 in.
Description: Gray fur, long,
pointy, pinkish nose, white
face, large ears and round na-
ked tail.
Where to find: Forests and
usually near water.
Note: Carries young in pouch.
Our only marsupial is related
to Australia's kangaroo.

COTTONTAIL RABBIT
Sylvilagus floridanus
Size: From 13 to 16 in. Tail, 2 in.
Description: Tan with darker hairs, short front legs and long, strong back legs. White puff for tail.
Where to find: Brush and forest edges.

RIVER OTTER
Lontica canadensis
Size: From 20 to 35 in.
Tail, 10–18 in.
Description: Weasel-like shape. Dark brown fur, often with golden gloss. Thick furry tail tapering toward tip. Webbed toes.
Where to find: Along rivers and streams.
Note: Recent restoration efforts have increased otter numbers in many parts of Missouri.

STRIPED SKUNK
Mephitis mephites
Size: From 15 to 19 in.
Tail, 7–10 in.
Description: Black with white facial stripe and neck patch. White on back. Mottled, bushy tail.
Where to find: Open forest and brushy areas.
Note: Omits poignant stench when threatened—**Be careful!**

BEAVER

Castor canadensis

Size: From 27 to 38 in. Tail, 9–12 in.

Description: Brown fur, prominent front teeth, tail is large, paddle-like and scaly.

Where to find: Lakes and streams, close to birches, poplars or food trees.

Note: Tremendous dam-building abilities. Look for cone-shaped tree stumps and, if you find one, take note of the coloration. If the inner bark is still green and fresh it may be a work in progress. Along the large rivers, piles of edible branches are often stored in the water for use in the winter. Homes are built in the riverbanks. Beaver dens can often be smelled before sighted. The musky odor will alert you to their presence.

WOODCHUCK *or* **GROUNDHOG**

Marmota monax

Size: From 14 to 20 in. Tail, 4–6 in.

Description: Gray-brown, large head, chunky body, short legs and small bushy tail.

Where to find: Brushy areas. Lives in burrows.

RACCOON
Procyon lotor
Size: From 16 to 26 in. Tail, 8–12 in.
Description: Bushy ringed tail and dark eye mask.
Where to find: Streams, rocky bluffs and usually near water.
Note: Raccoons wash everything they eat.

RED FOX
Vulpes vulpes
Size: From 20 to 30 in. Tail, 14–16 in.
Description: Reddish on back and face. White in belly. Bushy tail is white-tipped. Black legs and feet.
Where to find: Forests with open areas and farmlands.

GRAY FOX
Urocyon cinereoargenteus
Size: From 22 to 30 in. Tail, 10–15 in.
Description: Salt-and-pepper gray-orange with white markings. Tail is bushy, black-tipped with black stripe on top.
Where to find: Open woodlands, hollow logs and tree trunks.
Note: Can climb trees.

BOBCAT
Lynx rufus
Size: From 26 to 46 in. Tail, 5 in.
Description: Fur is golden brown with spotted belly. Short tail, black on top only.
Where to find: Caves, hollow logs and rocky ledges.
Note: Not seen very often. Dens often smell musky.

COYOTE
Canis latrans
Size: From 32 to 40 in. Tail, 12–15 in.
Description: Gray with tawny legs, feet and ears. Tail held between legs when running.
Where to find: Brush, open forests and prairies.

WHITE-TAILED DEER
Odocoileus virginianus
Size: From 4 to 6 ft. Tail, 8–12 in.
Description: Gold-gray-brown. Tail white on underside, raised when alarmed. Male has antlers that are reddish in summer and grayish-brown in winter. Antlers drop in late winter.

Where to find: Brushy areas and forests.
Note: Early morning and dusk are best the best times to see them. Bent or nibbled branches may indicate that deer have been browsing.

Reptiles & Amphibians

Snakes

F ew people are actually bitten by snakes, and most bites that do occur are the result of people trying to handle or kill a snake. In fact, more people die from dog bites, bee stings, lightning and falling off ladders than from snake bites.

When you sight a snake, stay calm. Remember—they are usually just as scared of you as you are of them. They are not to be feared or bothered. Use common sense. Avoid a snake you can't identify. Be careful around areas like swamps, marshes and bluffs. To be extra cautious, wear protective footwear such as tall hiking shoes and don't place your hands under rocks or logs. Also, look the ground over you're hiking, especially when you stop to stand or sit. Snakes are truly interesting and important components of the river valley ecosystem.

Where and When to Observe Snakes

M any types of snakes are found in the Missouri River valley. Snakes are commonly found near the edges of streams, rivers, ponds and lakes. Rocky bluffs and tangles of timber are favorite haunts, along with bogs, marshes and wetlands.

Snakes are primarily nocturnal creatures. However, because they are cold-blooded (ectotherms), snakes can be found during the day sunning on rocks. As the temperature increases, the early morning hours of summer days become prime snake-spotting times. In anticipation of their upcoming winter hibernation, snakes take advantage of mild fall weather and are increasingly more active during the daylight hours.

All about Snakes

The Missouri River valley is home to many snakes. Scientists that study reptiles and amphibians are herpetologists. Statewide there are 52 species and subspecies of these fascinating reptiles. All snakes should be treated with respect, even though only 5 species found in Missouri are venomous. Snakes have some distinct features that are worth noting:

- Snakes have translucent scales that cover their eyelids—their eyelids are fixed and not movable.

- Snakes lack external ear openings—they "hear" by sensing vibration.

- Snakes move by flexing their bodies, which contain a complex system of vertebrae (typically 200–400)—all snakes can swim.

- Snakes feed by swallowing their food whole and, with the exception of the venomous and constrictor varieties, eat their prey alive.

- Snakes use their forked tongues to detect smells.

- Snakes shed the outer layer of their skins as they grow—typically several times a year. Discarded snake skins are always inside out and are usually transparent.

A Sample Entry for Snakes

COMMON NAME
Scientific Name
Size: Indicates adult from tip of snout to vent—this is measured in a straight line.
Description: Coloration and identifying marks.
Where to find: Most common habitats and areas where likely to be spotted.
Note: May include other local names, interesting facts or trivia.

BULLSNAKE
Pituophis melanoleucus sayi
Size: From 50 to 72 in.
Description: Tan with many brown or black markings. Tail may have light or dark bands.
Where to find: Prairies, dense grassy areas in open spaces or in animal burrows.
Note: This is Missouri's largest snake and valued for its ability to control rodent populations. Kills its prey by constriction.

KINGSNAKE
Lampropeltis calligaster calligaster
Size: From 30 to 42 in.
Description: Tan to brown or greenish-gray covered with blotchy brown markings.

Where to find: Prairies and open woods.
Note: Known for their ability to eat other snakes, including venomous ones. Often mistaken for copperheads. Kingsnakes have round markings on their backs whereas copperheads have hourglass markings.

SPECKLED SNAKE
Lampropeltis getulus holbrooki
Size: From 36 to 48 in.
Description: Black with small white and yellow spots, making it look speckled.
Where to find: Secretive and rocky wooded hillsides.
Note: Also known as the Salt and Pepper Snake. Like all other Missouri kingsnakes, it vibrates its tail when threatened or disturbed.

BLACK or **RAT SNAKE**
Elaphe obsoleta obsoleta
Size: From 42 to 72 in.
Description: Shiny black. Belly is
mottled gray and black. Young are
light green or cream with dark brown
and black markings.
Where to find: Wooded hillsides,
wooded areas along rivers and near
farm buildings.
Note: One of the largest common
snakes. Record length is 7 ft. Can
climb trees. Kills its prey by constriction.

GARTER SNAKE
Thamnophis sirtalis sirtalis
Size: From 18 to 26 in.
Description: Color varies. Dark
brown, gray or olive with yellowish stripes. Belly is yellow-
ish-green.
Where to find: Meadows and
along streams.
Note: Will bite to defend itself.
Secretes a foul-smelling musk
from glands at the base of the
tail when first captured.

WATER SNAKE
Nerodia sipedon sipedon
Size: From 24 to 42 in.
Description: Gray to reddish-
brown. Dark brown cross bands.
Belly is cream-colored with dark
half-moon markings
Where to find: Sloughs, along riv-
ers, marshes, ponds and lakes.
Note: Will bite to defend itself, but

is harmless. Is often mistaken for a
Cottonmouth or Water Moccasin, a dangerously venomous species that can deliver a fatal bite. But Water Moccasins are found only in southeastern Missouri
and in the southern Ozarks.

HOGNOSE SNAKE
Heterodon platyrhinos
Size: From 20 to 33 in.
Description: Gray-brown to tan, dark brown markings on its back. Belly is mottled with gray.
Where to find: Sandy areas and open woods, needs loose soil.
Note: Can hiss loudly and spread its neck like a cobra. Can also play dead, flipping on its back and vomiting. Known in different locals as Spreadhead, Puff Adder or Hissing Viper.

RED MILK SNAKE
Lampropeltis getulus holbrooki
Size: From 21 to 28 in.
Description: White to light tan, bright red or orange markings with black borders.
Where to find: Under rocks on wooded hillsides and cedar groves.

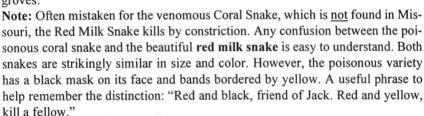

Note: Often mistaken for the venomous Coral Snake, which is <u>not</u> found in Missouri, the Red Milk Snake kills by constriction. Any confusion between the poisonous coral snake and the beautiful **red milk snake** is easy to understand. Both snakes are strikingly similar in size and color. However, the poisonous variety has a black mask on its face and bands bordered by yellow. A useful phrase to help remember the distinction: "Red and black, friend of Jack. Red and yellow, kill a fellow."

RINGNECK SNAKE
Diadophis punctatus arnyi
Size: From 10 to 24 in.
Description: Uniform gray to grayish-brown or black with yellow-orange belly. Yellow ring around its neck.
Where to find: Under rocks on rocky wooded hillsides.
Note: A very reclusive and secretive snake that not only hides for protection but feeds on small insects and other animals that are common to such places.

Poisonous Snakes

The skill of identifying poisonous snakes is an important one. In order to remain safe during your outdoor excursions, learn to identify the poisonous snakes you are likely to encounter.

Familiarize yourself with the size, coloration and likely habitats of the poisonous snakes. Here are some additional tips to help you to distinguish the potentially harmful varieties:

- Missouri's venomous snakes are all pit vipers, that is, they have openings on each side of their heads called *sensory pits*. Harmless snakes lack this distinctive feature.

- During daylight hours, the pupil can be used to differentiate poisonous and harmless snake types. All venomous snakes have vertical, slit-like pupils. In contrast, round pupils identify harmless snakes.

- Although venomous snakes do have triangle-shaped heads, many harmless snakes can adapt their head and neck shapes when alarmed so that they, too, often appear triangular. Consequently, this is not a reliable means of identification.

COMMONLY SEEN POISONOUS SNAKES

COPPERHEAD
Agkistrodon contortrix phaeogaster
Size: From 24 to 36 in.
Description: Pinkish-tan to grayish-brown with hour-glass-shaped cross bands of dark gray, brown or reddish-brown. Head is often a pink-orange color. Tail is yellow or greenish-yellow, especially when young.
Where to find: Rocky hillsides, brushy edges of forests and along prairie streams.
Note: Missouri's most common venomous snake. Will vibrate tail when alarmed. Does not kill, but the bite does require medical treatment as soon as possible.

TIMBER RATTLESNAKE
Crotalus horridus
Size: From 36 to 54 in. Missouri's largest venomous snake.
Description: Tan or yellowish-tan with dark brown markings on the back that change to bands near the tail. Often has a rust-colored stripe down the back and a large rattle at the end of its tail.
Where to find: Rocky and wooded hillsides, especially south-facing areas.
Note: Extremely venomous. Prompt medical treatment required.

The **Osage Copperhead** and **Timber Rattlesnake** are the only poisonous snakes common to the Missouri River valley. Three other poisonous species are found elsewhere in Missouri: Western Cottonmouth (Water Moccasin), Western Pygmy Rattlesnake (Ground Rattler) and Eastern Massasauga Rattlesnake (Swamp Rattler).

Snake Bite First Aid

S nake bites are not generally life-threatening. If you follow the suggestions provided in this guidebook you will greatly reduce your chances of getting bitten. But, if you do get bitten, here are some tips on what to do next:

If you are bitten by a non-venomous snake you need only treat the bite as you would a small wound. Clean the bite area with soap and water (you should try to use water from a water bottle), dry the skin and apply an adhesive bandage. The bite should heal nicely and you need only try to keep the area clean and dry.

Bites from poisonous snakes are also generally <u>NOT</u> life-threatening. However, they do require prompt medical treatment. The key to treatment is beginning the correct treatment immediately.

Here are the steps to follow:

1. Have the victim lie down. Keep the victim calm and quiet and position the area of the bite lower than the rest of the body.

2. If possible, wash the wound with clean water.

3. The victim should be treated for shock. The symptoms of shock can be lessened by talking calmly, keeping the victim warm and encouraging small sips of water.

4. Get the victim to a doctor as soon as possible.

DO NOT DO ANY OF THE FOLLOWING:
Do not apply ice
Do not cut the wound
Do not apply a tourniquet

If you are traveling solo, keep in mind that you will be responsible for getting yourself to medical care. Refer to the above list and be sure to remain calm. Although time should not be wasted in finding assistance, slow and steady progress will help keep you safe.

One addition note: Commercial snakebite kits are available and often do an effective job of lessening the severity of a bite—they are, however, no substitute for prompt medical attention.

LIZARDS

Lizards, much like snakes, are often feared and misunderstood. These important reptiles are common here and are valued, in addition to their beauty, for their insect-hunting abilities and importance in the food chain.

Lizards are typically long and slender. Most have 4 legs while one species found in Missouri has none. Lizards are covered with dry scales and have claws on their toes. They are commonly found in warm, dry habitats. None are venomous, although they will bite to defend themselves if captured. Unlike snakes, lizards have movable eyelids and ear openings.

These active reptiles are fun to spot and watch. They are especially active in early spring following their winter hibernation. Lizards prefer sunny days and, during cooler or cloudy weather, will most often remain hidden under cover.

With their bright colors and curious habits, lizards are fun to watch. Remember that lizards are harmless and important members of the natural community. They should not be feared or killed.

LIZARDS & THEIR TAILS

Why do they fall off? Will they grow back?
Do they sting?

Most lizards have relatively long, harmless tails—they are definitely not used to sting! The tail is often very fragile and apt to break off if the lizard is caught. Once lost, a new but usually much shorter tail will grow back. The regenerated tail often differs in color and scale pattern from the original.

FENCE LIZARD
Sceloporus undulatus hyacinthinus
Size: From 4 to 7 in.
Description: Rough scales, brown to gray with dark and light stripes or wavy crossbars. Males have blue patches on throat and belly.
Where to find: On fences or trees near dry woodlands, prairies and in brush.
Note: Excellent climbers. Often scurry up trees to escape predators.

BLUE-TAILED SKINK
Eumeces fasciatus
Size: From 5 to 8 in.
Description: Slender body. Adult has gray tail, young has blue tail. Both are striped.
Where to find: In leaf litter and shaded spots.
Note: Often runs extremely fast on warm days. Also called the Five-Lined Skink.

TURTLES

G ive turtles a chance. They are among the oldest groups of reptiles on earth. Turtles are divided into 3 groups: hard-shelled aquatic turtles, soft-shelled aquatic turtles and hard-shelled land turtles. All Missouri turtles lay their eggs on land. They eat water plants, dead animals, snails, aquatic insects and crayfish. Turtles do not have teeth, rather, they have a beak that allows them to use their jaws like scissors to bite off bits of food.

Look for turtles sunning themselves on the exposed surfaces of logs and in the shallow waters along streams and other bodies of water. Turtles, like most reptiles, are cold-blooded and rely on outside sources such as direct sunlight or the heat retained in shallow water (warmed also by the sun) to maintain their body heat. Biologists label turtles and other reptiles ectotherms, since they cannot derive and maintain their own body heat.

In addition to the heat turtles retain from basking in the sun, these interesting reptiles use the ultraviolet (UV) radiation of the sun to generate vitamin D—an important vitamin that turtles require to digest food properly. Since a turtle's shell does not contain a significant blood supply, you will often see turtles lying in the sun with their head, neck and legs extended in order to maximize their UV exposure.

Some turtles carry salmonella, so be sure and wash after handling, especially young turtles. If seen on the road, moving them to the side they face could save them. Swimmers should not fear turtles. They won't bite unless picked up.

Turtles make poor pets. Taking a baby turtle home as a souvenir generally means sentencing the reptile to slow starvation. They are wild animals and should be left in their natural habitats.

A Sample Entry for Turtles

COMMON NAME
Scientific Name
Size: Size of adult measured from end to end along the midline of the bottom of the shell.
Description: Coloration and identifying marks.
Where to find: Most common habitats.
Note: Interesting facts or trivia.

BOX TURTLE
Terrapene carolina triunguis
Size: From 4 1/2 to 5 in.
Description: Olive or olive brown with faint yellow lines. Three toes on each hind foot.
Where to find: Likes oak or hickory forests and brush.
Note: Can pull itself entirely into its shell.

MAP TURTLE
Graptemy pseudogeographica
Size: From 6 to 10 in.
Description: Center of shell is ridged. Backward L-shaped yellow line behind each eye. Yellow eyes with round black pupils.
Where to find: Rivers, sloughs, oxbow lakes and man-made water areas.
Note: Often basks in areas with thick aquatic vegetation.

SOFTSHELL TURTLE
Trionyx muticus muticus
Size: From 5 to 7 in.
Description: As the name implies, this turtle lacks a hard shell. Olive gray or brown upper shell with faint markings of dots and dashes. Lower shell is

cream color. Head and limbs are olive or gray on top and light gray or cream below. A light yellow line bordered by black is usually behind each eye. It has a very pointed "nose."
Where to find: Large rivers and streams where sand or mud is abundant.
Note: You may sometimes view just the head protruding from the water.

PAINTED TURTLE
Chrysemys picta belli
Size: From 5 to 7 in.
Description: Dark olive with faint yellow spaces, irregular lines. Reddish-orange outer edge on shell. Head and legs will be dark brown or black and strongly patterned with yellow lines. Looks "painted."

Where to find: Slow-moving water, ponds and drainage ditches. Needs ample mud and abundant aquatic vegetation. Likes to bask in the sun on logs and half-submerged rocks or along banks.

Note: Commonly seen in ditches along the Katy Trail State Park.

RED-EARED SLIDER
Chrysemy scripta elegans
Size: From 5 to 8 in.
Description: Olive brown with black and yellow lines. Red or orange stripe on each side of the head behind the eye.
Where to find: Rivers, sloughs, oxbow lakes and other lakes and ponds.
Note: Depleted in many areas due to over-collection for the pet trade.

SNAPPING TURTLE
Chelydra serpentina serpentina
Size: From 8 to 12 in. Can range from 10 to 25 lb.
Description: Gray-brown hard shell but often covered with mud or algae. Very large and aggressive.
Where to find: Near waterways.
Note: Considered a game species. Many have been captured and eaten by people. Many scientists believe their numbers are becoming reduced. This turtle can inflict a painful bite. It also has very sharp claws.

FROGS, TOADS & SALAMANDERS

F rogs and toads make up nearly 85 percent of all the species of amphibians. Frogs and toads differ from salamanders by having relatively short bodies and no tails as adults. However, like all amphibians, frogs and toads live their lives in 2 stages: an aquatic larval stage (tadpole) and a semi-aquatic or terrestrial stage.

Frogs and toads are common along the Missouri River. Forests and prairies, ponds and rivers, streams and swamps typically provide suitable homes for frogs and toads—they can be found almost everywhere! Look and listen as you pass through these areas—you are sure to encounter one or more species of frog or toad. Dusk, especially in the warmer days of spring and summer, is a prime time to listen to the vocal performances (often choruses) of these creatures.

Typically, only the males vocalize. Their calls frequently can be heard for miles and can be roughly divided into four categories: (1) mating calls, (2) release calls, (3) territorial calls and (4) warning calls.

Frogs and toads play important roles as both predators and prey in the various food chains of the region. Frogs and toads primarily feed on insects and, as a result of their keen harvesting abilities, are extremely valuable natural resources that help to keep the insect populations in check.

Although a primary food source for many snakes, fish, turtles and even some mammals, frogs and toads have a unique characteristic that helps them avoid becoming appetizers. Both secrete foul-flavored substances from their skin when they are seized by predators. These unpleasant and irritating secretions decrease their appeal to some predators. This is especially true for toads, whose secretions are particularly strong and pungent. People are normally not affected, although human eyes are sensitive to these substances. That is why it is important to wash your hands after handling a toad or frog. Despite what your mother told you, toads **DO NOT** cause warts.

FROG OR TOAD
WHICH IS IT?

Frogs and toads are very similar, but there are some key differences. The following characteristics should help you make the correct identification:

- Frog have smooth wet skin. Toads have warty, dry skin.
- Frogs have tiny teeth. Toads do not have teeth.
- Frogs jump. Toads hop.
- Frogs lay their eggs in clumps, clusters, or thin films.
- Female toads lay their eggs in parallel strings.
- Frogs typically have longer hind legs than toads.

A SAMPLE ENTRY
FOR FROGS, TOADS & SALAMANDERS

COMMON NAME
Scientific Name
Size: Indicates size of adult measured from tip of snout to vent.
Description: Coloration and identifying marks.
Where to find: Gives most common habitats.
Note: May include other local names, interesting facts or trivia.

GRAY TREEFROG
Hyla chrysoscelis
and *Hyla versicolor*
Size: From 1 1/4 to 2 in.
Description: Gray, greenish-gray or brown, sometimes bright green. There is always a white marking below each eye.
Where to find: They breed in late May and early June in fishless, woodland ponds, then move into forested areas.
Note: Missouri's most common species of tree frog. Can sound like a buzzer or have a bird-like, musical trill depending on species.

SPRING PEEPER
Hyla crucifer crucifer
Size: From 3/4 to 1 1/4 in.
Description: Gray to light tan tree frog with a dark X on its back.
Where to find: Woodlands, stagnant water and thick undergrowth.
Note: Listen for it in early spring on warm nights. Characteristic high-pitched, peeping call.

PLAINS LEOPARD FROG
Rana blairi
Size: From 2 to 3 3/4 in.
Description: Tan, with round brown, olive or dark green spots on back.
Where to find: Ponds, marshes and flooded fields.
Note: Makes a "chuck-chuck" sound.

SOUTHERN LEOPARD FROG
Rana sphenocephala
Size: From 2 to 3 1/2 in.
Description: Like Plains Leopard Frog but green on back.
Where to find: Ponds, marshes, flooded areas.
Note: Makes a chuckle-like "quack-quack" sound.

BULLFROG
Rana catesbeiana
Size: From 3 1/2 to 6 in.
Description: Green to olive to brown. Similar to but larger than Green Frog.
Where to find: Marshes, sloughs, ponds, lakes, rivers and creeks.
Note: Largest Missouri species of frog. Makes "jug-o-rum" sound.

AMERICAN TOAD
Bufo americanus americanus
Size: From 2 to 3 1/2 in.
Description: Gray, light brown or reddish-brown. The belly is cream-colored and mottled with dark gray. Has warts and a large visible gland behind each eye.
Where to find: Near woodland ponds or water-filled ditches. Often on land.
Note: Call is a high-pitched trill.

Salamanders

S alamanders are seldom encountered because of their habits. They are generally small in size, are reclusive and move slowly. To even the most diligent naturalist, these interesting amphibians often prove extremely hard to find.

Distinguishing between salamanders and lizards can often be confusing. However, unlike lizards, salamanders typically have moist, smooth skin and their toes lack claws. Salamanders share the ability of lizards to regenerate a lost tail—this is a common defense mechanism that aids these creatures when they are trapped.

Salamanders require moisture and generally avoid exposure to direct sunlight. They prefer cooler temperatures and are therefore generally most active during the spring and fall. Most are nocturnal and can most often be found under rocks, fallen limbs or other protective cover.

SPOTTED SALAMANDER
Ambystoma maculatum
Size: From 5 to 9 in. Stout lizard-like body.
Description: Dark brown to black, with 2 rows of orange or orange-yellow spots down the back.
Where to find: Near water along woods and hillsides.
Note: Large numbers are seen during early, warm spring rains.

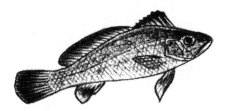

Fish

M issouri's waters are home to more than 200 species of fish. Fish are valuable members in the ever-changing river valley ecosystem. Fish are also important sources of food and recreational enjoyment for the state's many anglers.

All fish live in water, "breathe" through gills and have fins instead of legs. Most have scales that cover their bodies. Fish are vertebrates—so all fish have vertebral columns, or backbones.

Scientists that study fish are called ichthyologists.

A Sample Entry for Fish

COMMON NAME
Scientific Name
Size: Represents the size range of mature fish measured from tip of snout to end of tail (fins pressed together).
Weight: Range of average weight. May indicate state record.
Description: Body type, coloration and identifying marks.
Where to find: Gives most common habitats.
Note: May include other local names, interesting facts or trivia.

CARP

Cyprinus carpio
Size: From 12 to 25 in.
Weight: From 1 to 8 lb.
State record: 47 lb 7 oz.
Description: Long dorsal fin. Back and sides are olive in color. Belly is yellow-white. Black-brown tips on scales. Often red tip on tail fin and lower fins.
Where to find: Common to lakes, rivers and streams. May feed in shallow waters, but are primarily bottom feeders.
Note: Also known as German carp or European carp.

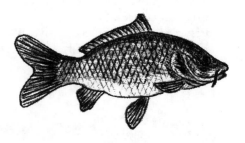

The **common carp** is an abundant and adaptable fish. Known for their fighting ability, these fish are also aggressive feeders. Most often caught with spinning gear (tight-line technique) or by jug fishing. Anglers frequently use doughball baits or earthworms—artificial baits can also be used. Relatively small hooks are recommended due to their small mouths. Dawn and from of June through September are the best times to catch these formidable game fish.

CHANNEL CATFISH

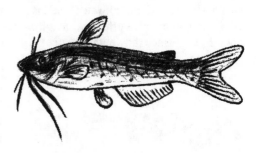

Ictalurus punctatus
Size: From 12 to 32 in.
Weight: From 1 to 15 lb.
State record: 34 lb 10 oz.
Description: Back and sides olive brown or gray-blue often with accompanying black spots. White belly. Yellow-brown fins. Enlarged fleshy head with thick lips.
Where to find: Rivers, streams, lakes and ponds. Occur in a variety of Missouri aquatic habitats.
Note: Known locally as Spotted Cat, Blue Cat or Chucklehead Cat. Among Missouri's most commonly caught sport fish.

Large adult **channel catfish** tend to prefer large, deep pools. During the day, they feed in deep water or rest around and under heavy submerged cover. Feeding tends to increase at dusk, and night often draws them to shallower water. Although known to feed on a wide variety of insects, these fish are not picky eaters. Smaller fish, plants, worms and crayfish are just some of the more common elements in their diets. Common angling methods include tight-lines, limb-lines and trotlines.

Since **channel catfish** feed primarily by scent, strong-smelling baits such as chicken liver, pieces of shad, crayfish, worms and commercial stink bait are excellent choices. Small spinners and spoons are artificial lures that, when retrieved slowly, are often effective. When fished near the bottom, these tackle and bait combinations typically produce good results. Although active year-round, the warmer summer months often yield the largest number of catches.

BLUE CATFISH
Ictalurus furcatus
Size: From 20 to 44 in.
Weight: From 3 to 40 lb.
Description: Head is distinctively wedge-shaped. Lack the dark spots on back and sides that are characteristic of channel catfish.

Where to find: Missouri and Mississippi Rivers and their major tributaries. They prefer swift water and are found near the bottoms or in the midwater of major channels.
Note: Other local names include Blue Fultons or White Cats.

Blue catfish are commonly found in the swift current of major channels or near channel borders. Light saltwater tackle is recommended, although trotlines loaded with live bait are also effective. Skipjack herring and cut gizzard shad produce good results, since they both produce oils that are attractive to catfish.

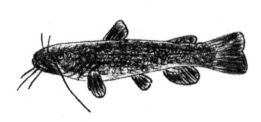

FLATHEAD CATFISH
Pylodictis olivaris
Size: From 15 to 45 in.
Weight: From 1 to 45 lb.
State record: 66 lb.
Description: Slender body. Flat, projecting head with prominent lower jaw. Body is often speckled with black or brown.

Where to find: Large streams and rivers. Prefer deep pools that have substantial current.
Note: Commonly called Yellow Cat, Goujon or Johnnie Cat.

Prized by anglers for their excellent flavor, **flathead catfish** are much sought-after river fish. Although a variety of methods can be used to harvest these fish, flathead catfish prefer live bait. Trotlines or tight-line setups loaded with large minnows, sunfish or goldfish typically are especially effective. Dusk and nighttime are the best times to fish for these cats. Deep, moving pools and borders of the channel current are good places to try your luck.

BLACK BULLHEAD
Ictalurus melas
Size: Up to 16 in.
Weight: Seldom exceed 2 1/2 lb.
Description: A pudgy catfish with slight notch in tailfin. Chin barbells are white. Yellowish-brown, olive or black back and sides. Belly is white or yellow.
Where to find: River backwaters and in pools of turbid streams and creeks. Prefers muddy, silt bottoms.
Note: Referred to locally as Mud Cat.

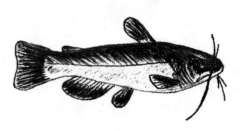

YELLOW BULLHEAD
Ictalurus natalis
Size: From 7 to 13 1/2 in.
Weight: To 1 1/2 lb.
Description: A pudgy catfish with nearly straight tailfin. Chin barbells are white. Yellowish-brown back and sides. Belly is white or yellow.
Where to find: River backwaters and in pools of turbid streams and creeks. Prefers muddy, silt bottoms.
Note: Referred to locally as Yellow Cat.

Both the **black bullhead** and the **yellow bullhead** are common in the Missouri River valley; however the latter is significantly less abundant. These bottom feeders can be fished using earthworms, crayfish, frogs and chicken livers. The most common way to catch bullheads is to fish these natural baits on or near the bottom from a cane pole or rod and reel.

FRESHWATER DRUM
Aplodinotus grunniens
Size: From 12 to 20 in.
Weight: From 1 to 5 lb.
Description: Gray dorsal ridge and silvery sides.
Where to find: Large rivers, streams and deeper waters of big lakes. A bottom-feeder.

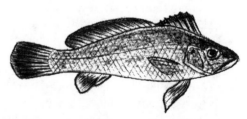

Note: Gets its name from the grunting sounds it produces. Large numbers in the Missouri River. Local names include Gaspergou, Croaker or Silver Bass.

Swift water provides the principal habitat for **freshwater drum**. This fish stays close to the bottom and uses its head to rustle up crayfish, mollusk and aquatic insects. Crayfish, worm and minnows are solid natural baits. Artificial tackle such as spinners and wet flies are also known to produce consistent catches.

Fish

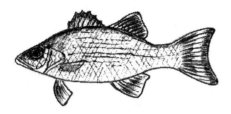

WHITE BASS
Morone chrysops
Size: From 9 to 15 in.
Weight: From 1/4 to 1 1/4 lb. (may grow as large as 5 lb.)
Description: Spiny rays. Silver with black horizontal streaks along the sides. Stripes may appear olive gray.
Where to find: Big rivers, lakes and reservoirs. Common to clearer, moving waters that pass over sandy or rocky bottoms.
Note: Known also as Stripers or Silver Bass.

White bass are relatively new to the Missouri River. Early spring, midsummer and late fall provide anglers with good fishing opportunities. Minnows are often the preferred live bait and many anglers use artificial tackle. Jig, plugs and spoons are recommended. Since these fish are sight feeders, many indicate that white is the best color. Low, clear water conditions often produce good results.

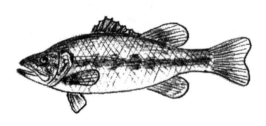

LARGEMOUTH BASS
Micropterus salmoides
Size: From 10 to 20 in.
Weight: From 1/2 to 4 1/2 lb.
State record: 13 lb 14 oz.
Description: Slender sunfish with an enlarged mouth. Upper jaw extends beyond the eye. Greenish upper parts with silver or brassy body with distinctive broad and continuous black stripe. Belly is white.
Where to find: Rivers, lakes, streams and farm ponds. Prefer warmer waters that lack strong currents. Frequent around large rock structures or heavy natural cover.
Note: Local names include Bigmouth Bass, Mossback or Lineside Bass.

Due to their wide distribution and great fighting characteristics, **largemouth bass** are among the most important sport fishes in North America. These attractive game fish are taken throughout the year, with the preferred angling times being the warmer months of late spring, summer and early fall. A wide variety of baits can be used successfully to catch these fish. Natural baits include frogs, minnows and worms. Artificial lures such as flies, jigs, surface plugs, spinners and spoons are commonly used to take largemouth bass. Daytime and evening offers good angling opportunities. Largemouth bass are often found in deeper, off-channel water in the day where they lurk near logs, drift piles and other types of cover. During the evening hours, they are commonly abundant in shallow water among heavy cover and rocky ledges.

BLUEGILL
Lepomis macrochirus
Size: Up to 9 1/2 in.
Weight: Average 12 oz.
State record: 3 lb.
Description: Small mouth. Jaw does not pass the eye. Back and sides are dark olive green and often marked with vertical dark bars. Belly is yellow or reddish-orange. Lower lip and gill covers are characteristically blue.
Where to find: Floodplains of major rivers, streams, lakes and ponds.
Note: Missouri's most abundant sunfish. Local names include Sun Perch and Pond Perch.

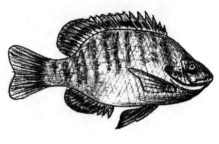

Bluegill share habitats that are similar to those of the largemouth bass and, where you find one, you will often find the other. Mid-May to mid-June is a prime time to harvest bluegill as this marks their yearly spawning season; however, they can be taken year-round. Earthworms, crickets, grasshoppers and mealworms are good natural baits. Jig, flies or small spinners make good artificial baits. Bluegill are commonly taken in off-channel waters, sloughs, chutes and tributaries.

WHITE CRAPPIE
Pomoxis annularis
Size: Up to 15 1/2 in.
Weight: Seldom exceeds 2 lb.
State record: 4 lb 5 oz.
Description: Dark olive back with purple reflections. Silver sides with black tints arranged in discontinuous vertical bands.
Where to find: Deeper pools of rivers, streams, lakes and reservoirs. Common in off-channel waters of major rivers.
Note: Locally known as Calico Bass, Slabs or Tinmouth.

BLACK CRAPPIE
Pomoxis nigromaculatus
Size: To 14 1/2 in.
Weight: To 1 lb. 12 oz. (May grow to 4 lb)
Description: Dark olive on top. Silver sides with dark black spot. Black marks do not form vertical bars.
Where to find: Deeper pools of rivers, streams, lakes and reservoirs. Common in off-channel waters of major rivers.
Note: Not as widely distributed as white crappie.

Both the **white crappie** and **black crappie** vary their habitats according to the season. During the winter, crappie tend to reside near deep water structures. As the water levels and temperatures rise, crappie move into shallow water of off-channel areas. Throughout the summer months, they inhabit the cooler water of the main channel border. Cooler autumn weather drives crappie back to tributaries and off-channel areas. Both varieties are frequently caught using small live minnows. Artificial lures such as jigs and spinners are also effective.

WALLEYE
Stizostedion vitreum
Size: From 12 to 28 in.
Weight: From 8 oz. to 8 lb.
State record: 21 lb 1 oz.
Description: Olive brown or yellowish back and sides. Marked with dark blotches. Also has a white belly.
Where to find: Rivers, large streams, lakes.
Note: Also called Jack Salmon or Walleyed Pike.

SAUGER
Stizostedion canadense
Size: Up to 18 in.
Weight: Rarely exceed 2 1/2 lb.
Description: Brown back and sides. Characteristically has 4 oblique dark spots on body. White belly. Dorsal fin has dark brown spots.
Where to find: Rivers and larger streams. Tolerant of fairly turbid and swift-moving water.
Note: Other local names include Spotted Jack, Sand Pike or Jack Salmon.

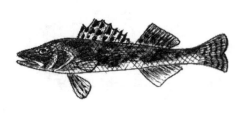

Walleye and **sauger** are large, fun to catch and great-tasting fish. These fish are commonly caught during the cooler days of late autumn and throughout the winter months. Preferred habitats include deep pools or channel borders that occur over rocky or debris-laden bottoms. Minnows are an attractive live bait, while crankbaits and jigs make good artificial lures. In addition to line-fishing, many anglers troll dikes and the margins between fast-moving and slower-moving water to harvest these attractive game fish.

Fishing Opportunities in the Missouri River Valley

Fishing is a logical way to further one's enjoyment along this natural corridor. The 14 species of fish presented in this guide offer a wide range of fishing opportunities and represent some of the major varieties that are commonly found in this region. You could easily take along 50 feet of 30-pound test line, some 1-ounce sinkers and some number 4 hooks and turn any ordinary afternoon into a small fishing expedition. A successful outing requires a good balance of fishing license, patience, luck and more patience. The easiest of these key ingredients to locate is the Missouri Fishing Permit, which is available at many gas stations and outdoor shops, especially near popular fishing spots. The patience is a little harder to come by...

The Flood of '93 cleaned out the river considerably and many people can be seen fishing up and down the Missouri. In addition to fishing the river, many have taken to seeking their bounties in the many recently formed "blue hole" lakes.

The first step toward making your river fishing trip a positive one is to leave your lightweight fishing rods and tackle at home. A strong river requires a strong rod or stick. The 30-pound test fishing line is recommended more for fighting snags than walleye. There are plenty of places along the river to get bait and a fishing license.

You can unspool your line and bank fish with a sturdy stick or "limb fish" from a hearty limb. Heavy sinkers allow the line to bury itself in the mud and a good 18-inch leader will allow your bait to float in the current.

Pollution and Fishing in the Missouri River Valley

The Missouri Department of Conservation has issued a health advisory that identifies many of the game fish found in the Missouri River and its tributaries to be potentially harmful. This advisory includes paddlefish, catfish, carp, buffalo, drum and suckers caught anywhere outside the Ozarks. The specifics of the advisory are contained in the *Wildlife Code* and these should be considered before consuming fish caught in the region.

For more information, contact:
Missouri Department of Conservation
Fisheries Advisory
P.O. Box 180
Jefferson City, MO 65102-0180
(573) 751-4115, ext. 175

All about
Catch-and-Release

A lthough many people fish Missouri rivers, streams and reservoirs to provide food for their tables, practicing catch-and-release is also a great way to
enjoy the sport. By releasing fish immediately back into the water after they are
caught, anglers can benefit from the experience and learn about the different
species of fish without decreasing the fish population. In fact, catch-and-release
fishing is a great way to increase fish populations. Here are some tips on catch-
and-release methods:

- When possible, do not remove the fish from the
water. This lessens the shock to the fish.

- Use barbless hooks. These hooks do not cause significant damage to the fish.

- Do not remove a hook that is lodged in a fish's
throat or stomach. It is better for the fish if you
simply cut the line. Most hooks will, with enough
time, deteriorate.

- Do not handle the fish excessively. Use the smallest amount of contact necessary to safely release
the fish.

- If you must handle your catch, make sure that you
do not squeeze or drop the fish.

- Do not stick your fingers in the fish's eyes or gills.

FISHING ACCESS POINTS

DEPARTMENT OF CONSERVATION
MISSOURI RIVER ACCESS AREAS

AREA	RIVER	COUNTY	FACILITIES
Blanchette Landing	Missouri	St. Charles	P, Cr, HT
Chamois	Missouri	Osage	P, Cr
Cooley Lake C.A.	Missouri	Clay	P, Cr
Franklin Island	Missouri	Howard	P, Cr, T
Hartsburg	Missouri	Boone	P, Cr, T
Hermann	Missouri	Gasconade	P, Cr, HT, HJ
Hoot Owl Bend	Missouri	Atchison	P
Howell Island	Missouri	St. Charles	P
Langdon Bend	Missouri	Atchison	P, Cr, T
Marion	Missouri	Cole	P, Cr, T
Miami Rvrfrnt Prk	Missouri	Saline	P, Cr, T
Mokane	Missouri	Callaway	P, Cr, T
New Haven	Missouri	Franklin	P, Cr
Nodaway Island	Missouri	Andrew	P, Cr, T
Paynes Landing	Missouri	Holt	P, Cr, T
Taylor's Landing	Missouri	Cooper	P, Cr, T
Thurnau C.A.	Missouri	Holt	P, Cr, T
Washington Park	Missouri	Franklin	P, Cr
Weldon Springs	Missouri	St. Charles	P, Cr, T
Worthwine Island	Missouri	Andrew	P

TRIBUTARIES			
Coulter's Landing	Boeuf Creek	Franklin	P, Cr, T
Capitol View	Cedar Creek	Callaway	P, Cr, HT
Piggs Landing	Fishing	Ray	P, Cr, T
Moreau-50	Moreau	Cole	P, Cr, T
Watson	Nishnabotna	Atchison	P, Cr, T
Bonnots Mill	Osage	Osage	P, Cr, T
Providence	Perche Creek	Boone	P, Cr, T

Facilities Key:

P - parking lot (gravel)
Cr - concrete ramp
T - toilet
HT - handicapped-accessible toilet
HJ - handicapped-accessible jetty

Fish Legally!

B efore baiting a hook, remember to consider the rules. Obtain the proper license and when you do, be sure to obtain a copy of the Wildlife Code of Missouri. Resident hunting permits are available for under $10 and children under the age of 16 or adults 65 and over are not required to purchase fishing licenses. Generally, fish in the Missouri River have open season—they can be fished year-round. However, there are important exceptions so be sure to follow all the rules and regulations contained in the Wildlife Code.

Licenses, copies of the Wildlife Code of Missouri and information about fishing opportunities in the region can be obtained through the Missouri Department of Conservation. Here is a list of some of the department's service centers:

COLUMBIA
Missouri Department of Conservation
Central District Office
1907 Hillcrest Drive
Columbia, MO 65201
(573) 884-6861

HANNIBAL
Missouri Department of Conservation
P.O. Box 428
Tower Plaza
655 Clinic Road
Hannibal, MO 63401
(573) 248-2530

JEFFERSON CITY
Missouri Department of Conservation
P.O. Box 180
2901 W. Truman Blvd.
Jefferson City, MO 65109
(573) 751-4115

KANSAS CITY
Missouri Department of
Conservation
Brywood Shopping Center
8616 E. 63rd St.
Kansas City, MO 64133
(816) 356-2280

ST. JOSEPH
Missouri Department of
Conservation
701 N.E. College Dr.
St. Joseph, MO 64507
(816) 271-3100

ST. LOUIS
Missouri Department of
Conservation
Powder Valley Conservation
Nature Center
11715 Cragwold Rd.
Kirkwood, MO 63122
(314) 301-1500

In addition to the outlets listed above, fishing licenses and copies of the Wildlife Code are available at many local gas stations, convenience stores and sporting goods stores. Licenses can also be obtained by calling: 1 (800) 392-4115. Good luck!

READING THE SKY

Reading the sky while on a hike is fun and can also be important when a change of weather is near. Here are a few of the major cloud and weather patterns you may encounter during your outings:

Cirrus and Cirrocumulus clouds are ice crystal clouds known as mares' tails because of their narrow, fluffy shapes. They are generally 20,000 to 30,000 feet up.

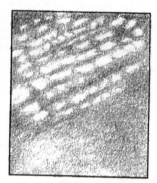

Altostratus clouds form at about 25,000 feet in thin pale gray sheets that still allow you to see the sun and moon but as if through clouded glass.

Altocumulus clouds are at about 15,000 to 20,000 feet and are more puffy, but have dark undersides. Sailors used to call it a mackerel sky because the underside of the clouds are in ripples and look like fish scales. This type of cloud also produces a pale blue or yellow corona that is reddish outside. This forms a much larger ring than the cirrostratus clouds.

Stratocumulus clouds are irregular puffy gray non-rain-producing clouds, but if they drop down, and fuse together, they can turn into rain-producing nimbostratus clouds. They are at about 6,000 to 10,000 feet above the ground.

Cumulus clouds only come on warm sunny days and often disappear at night. They are at 15,000 to 20,000 feet high

Cumulonimbus are clouds with a lot of up and down movement. They are large in size and can produce violent storms, even tornadoes. They form at about 12,000 feet above the ground but can rise to 75,000 feet and are often shaped like anvils.

Stratus clouds are in thick layers like fog, around 5,000 feet or even lower over the ground and are the producers of mist and drizzle.

Nimbostratus clouds at 3,000 feet or less are the major rain clouds. They are dark, look wet, and if you are in an open area, you can watch closely and often see long rain streaks coming from them. They are often accompanied by fat clouds called **scud clouds**.

Fog hugs the ground.
It is basically a cloud that you can walk through.

Dew is water vapor that condenses on solid surfaces that have cooled below the condensation point. It usually occurs on clear nights. Did you know the condensation on the outside of a glass of ice water is also dew?

Frost is formed like dew, except when temperatures fall below freezing, water vapor changes into ice crystals before condensing into water drops. Frost patterns develop on windows when the primary frost melts and then recrystallizes.

Weather Tips

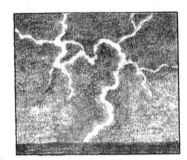

Lightning is the product of electrical energy in the atmosphere. This energy is released in channels that create brilliant and powerful lightning strikes. The best advice is to take cover and wait for the storm to pass. Never stand under a tree, especially a lone tree or in an open field. You can judge how many miles you are away from a thunderstorm by counting the seconds that pass as soon as you see the lightning until you hear the thunder. Then divide the total by five.

Floods form from fast-falling rain that can easily turn nearly dry little creeks into raging torrents. Plan for how to get out of harm's way if you choose to hike, bike or backpack and know it may rain or storm.

Squall Lines look like a wall of rolling, boiling black clouds and can be incredibly violent with rapidly shifting winds. They bring with them torrential rains and hail. Flash floods are common. Squall lines occur with the arrival of a cold front. It is good to seek cover when you see one approaching.

Tornadoes are violent whirlpools of air that look like a dipping, twisting, funnel-shaped cloud. Tornadoes occur because of instability in the air and are often accompanied by heavy thunderstorms and rain. They are generally quite noisy and come with cold fronts and squall lines. Though the path of destruction is usually fairly narrow, usually less than 1/8 of a mile, **BEWARE**, there may be more than one in a storm. If you see or hear one coming, seek immediate cover in a basement, storm cellar, ditch or other low area and protect your head.

Seven Spectacular
River Valley
Nature Trips

The following trips are places to start learning more about the Missouri River valley. They are all located along the Missouri River as it passes through the state of Missouri. They include Weston Bend State Park, Burr Oak Woods State Forest, Eagle Bluffs Conservation Area, Katy Trail, August A. Busch Conservation Area and Shaw Arboretum.

Nature trips and outings promote learning and provide the "hands-on, eyes-on, ears-on, senses-on" exposure that allows each of us to experience the Missouri River valley in our own special way. The six nature trips included in this guide were chosen for their general accessibility (you should be able to get to at least one of these areas in less than a few hours) and their unique features as representative "hot-spots" of Missouri River valley flora and fauna. This is by no means a definitive list but, rather, a helpful presentation of some places to expand, or perhaps begin, your understanding of the diversity within the river valley. Have fun and don't forget to ask, "What's that?"

If there is another river valley nature area closer to your home, call your local Department of Natural Resources or Conservation Department for tips. These agencies will be happy to provide you with information on state parks, conservation areas, fishing accesses and other nearby public lands. Also, many times local and national parks are highlighted on maps. Check the maps of your area to locate the parks and preserves nearest you. You can get a free Discover Outdoor Missouri Map from the Conservation Department by calling (573) 751-4115. For more information on the state of Missouri, contact the Division of Tourism at (573) 751-4133. For trip-planning information call 1 (800) 877-1234.

#1

WESTON BEND STATE PARK

2.5 miles south of Weston in Platte County, Missouri

Situated along the bluffs of the Missouri River in the northwestern corner of the state, Weston Bend State Park offers an exceptional display of river valley wild-life. Draped in loess soil and hemmed in by the Missouri River, Weston Bend State Park preserves a wide variety of flora and fauna that is representative of the valley's character in this region of the state. Existing today as a vibrant forest with interspersed ravines, minor valleys, prairies and bluffs, the terrain of the park is as interesting and diverse as the varieties of wildlife it supports. In addi-tion to the abundant opportunities for viewing and studying many different types of wildlife, a spectacular view of the "Mighty Mo" from a scenic overlook offers a unique view of the river. A paved three-mile loop trail courses through both forest and bluff-top landscapes and furnishes a rewarding nature experience for even the most convenience-minded naturalist. Weston Bend State Park offers ample hiking and biking opportunities, camping and picnicking facilities, mak-ing it a nature trip that should not be passed over.

Campsites – Picnic Areas – Shelters – Restrooms – Laundry – Hot Showers

Directions: The park is located just 40 miles northwest of Kansas City. From the north, take US 59 south from St. Joseph and continue for approximately 20 miles where US 59 heads west. Proceed south on MO 45 and in about 12 miles you will approach the park entrance. If coming from the south, take I-29 to Platte City. Turn west on MO 92 and go about 5 miles to MO 45. Proceed north on MO 45 and watch for the signs that lead to the park entrance.

For more information, contact:
Weston Bend State Park
Weston, MO 64098
(816) 640-5443

#2

BURR OAK WOODS STATE FOREST

18 miles east of downtown Kansas City
in Jackson County, Missouri

Conveniently located near Kansas City, the Burr Oak Woods State Forest provides a brilliant display of Missouri River valley wildlife. In addition to the 1,072 acres of valley forests, prairie, ponds and glades contained within its boundaries, the area is home to the Conservation Nature Center, which maintains wildlife displays and conducts a wide array of nature-study activities. The Nature Center also features a 3,000-gallon aquarium filled with native fish, turtles and many other aquatic creatures. Four trails: (1) Bethany Falls Trail, (2) Missouri Tree Trail, (3) Wildlife Habitat Trail and (4) Discovery Trail (paved), provide pathways to the enjoyment and study of representative Missouri River valley species.

Picnic Areas – Shelters – Restrooms

Directions: From I-70, exit north on Hwy. 70 (exit 20). Continue north on Hwy. 70 (approx. 1.5 miles) until you reach Park Road, turn left (west). The Nature Center and trailheads are located 1 mile along Park Road.

For more information, contact:
Burr Oak Woods Conservation Nature Center
Missouri Department of Conservation
1401 NW Park Road
Blue Springs, MO 64015
(816) 228-3766

#3

EAGLE BLUFFS CONSERVATION AREA

6 miles southwest of Columbia
near McBaine in Boone County, Missouri

The central location of this 4,269-acre wildlife area makes it a natural choice as a convenient site for exploring the Missouri River valley. In addition to its accessibility from I-70, Eagle Bluffs is bordered by the Katy Trail along its eastern boundary, which opens the area up to easy biking and hiking access as well. The area's 10 miles of frontage on the Missouri River and Perche Creek support a wide variety of wetland habitats that make sighting migratory and resident waterfowl very likely. In addition to the abundant waterfowl that often populate 1,250 acres of seasonal and emergent marshes, the area provides nature study possibilities for many representatives of the flora and fauna that are commonly found in the Missouri River valley. The entire area lends itself to nature study and fun. Birdwatching, hiking, fishing and photography are especially great ways to enjoy this area.

– Restrooms –

Directions: From I-70, go to Columbia and head south from the Providence Road exit on Providence Road. This road will take you through Columbia and all the way down to McBaine. Near McBaine on Route K, go 1 mile west on Burr Oak Road, then 2 miles south on Star School Road. In McBaine, Betty's Grill and Tavern can feed you and give you additional directions as well.

For more information, contact:
Eagle Bluffs Conservation Area
6700 W. Route K
Columbia, MO 65203
(573) 445-3882

EAGLE BLUFFS
A DIFFERENT TYPE
OF NATURE AREA

The Conservation Department purchased Eagle Bluffs Area to help reestablish the wetlands that were once so prevalent along the Missouri River. It has been estimated that more than 90 percent of the river valley's original wetlands have been lost due to river channelization, levees, drainage for agriculture and bank stabilization.

In an effort to reestablish these wetlands that are so needed by so many species, Conservation crews have recreated 13 shallow pools, using 16 miles of levees, 51 water control structures, river water supply pumps and a pipeline linking the area to the City of Columbia's wastewater treatment wetlands. In a unique cooperative project, the City of Columbia allows the Conservation Department to use treated wastewater as a primary water source for the wetlands. The end result of their effort has been the creation of the country's largest wetland area to use municipal wastewater to supplement a wetland's water requirements. By working in concert with the Missouri River and the normal rainfall of the region, the symbiotic arrangement between the City of Columbia and the Department of Conservation has produced a wildlife showcase that reflects and preserves the diversity of life that abounds in the Missouri River valley.

#4 ⚡ #5

KATY TRAIL STATE PARK

America's Longest Rails-to-Trails Project
Highlighted Trailheads: Rocheport and Weldon Spring

With the closure of the Missouri-Kansas-Texas Railroad in 1986, the Department of Natural Resources was able to secure the right-of-way for a rails-to-trails conversion where outdoor enthusiasts now enjoy all that the Missouri River valley has to offer. With its flat, crushed limestone surface and many convenient access points, the Katy Trail courses through dense forests, wetlands, deep valleys, open pastures and fields. The trail currently stretches close to 200 miles from Sedalia to St. Charles, and several extensions are currently under construction.

Directions to Rocheport Trailhead: Rocheport is centrally located halfway between Kansas City and St. Louis. Just 12 miles west of Columbia, it can be accessed from I-70. Take exit 115, go 2 miles north into town and follow the signs to the trailhead. This site offers easy access to tremendous river views, park benches and towering bluff lines.

Directions to Weldon Spring Trailhead: Go from Highway 40/61 to 94 west to D. Or, if coming from I-70, take 94 west to D. Both routes lead to the Weldon Spring Conservation Area—follow the signs to the trailhead. The trail here passes through dense forest, and the river is accessible from several gravel roads.

– Restrooms –

For more information, contact:
Katy Trail State Park, Missouri Department of Natural Resources
P.O. Box 180
Jefferson City, MO 65102
(573) 751-2479
or
Missouri Department of Natural Resources Information Hotline
1 (800) 334-6946

You can also receive a free color brochure on the Katy Trail from the Department of Natural Resources by calling toll-free 1 (800) 334-6946. Or, surf up the Missouri and visit the Interactive Katy Trail online, where it never rains! See the back of the book for more information. A free fold-out map of the entire Katy Trail is also available from Pebble Publishing by calling 1 (800) 576-7322.

#6

August A. Busch Memorial Conservation Area

30 miles northwest of St. Louis
at Weldon Spring in St. Charles County

Situated in the eastern section of the Missouri River valley, the August A. Busch Memorial Conservation Area provides a haven for many types of wildlife. Purchased from the federal government by the Missouri Department of Conservation in 1947 and located just north of the Missouri River, a 6,987-acre tract preserves much of the essence of the river valley landscape and wildlife. A collection of lakes, streams, wetlands, hillsides, prairies, and almost everything in between, makes this an important area to explore for naturalists seeking to learn more about the Missouri River. Rich in wildlife and habitat diversity, the area features many trails and access roads, which allow hikers to uncover the nature that abounds in habitats emerge in both upland and bottomland terrain. In addition to the hiking opportunities, the area features an 8.7-mile driving tour, a waterfowl refuge with a boardwalk, and regenerative prairies. The August A. Busch Memorial Conservation Area offers an exceptional and convenient look at a vast array of Missouri River valley habitats, terrain and wildlife that should be experienced—Don't forget to take along your nature guide!

Restrooms – Picnic Areas

Directions: Take U.S. Highway 40/61 to 94. Take 94 west for approximately half a mile to the entrance.

For more information, contact:
Missouri Department of Conservation
August A. Busch Memorial Conservation Area
2360 Highway D
St. Charles, MO 63304
(314) 441-4554

#7

Shaw Arboretum of the Missouri Botanical Garden

Located southwest of St. Louis
near Gray Summit in Franklin County

While not as close to the Missouri River as other natural areas mentioned in this guide, Shaw Arboretum is well worth a side trip. It is interesting that, within the Arboretum, the Meramec River reaches north to within 4 miles of the Missouri River—this is as close as the two rivers ever get. While conveniently located near St. Louis, the Arboretum has not lost its hold on protecting and preserving Missouri wildlife. The Aboretum features a 100-acre tall grass prairie, a 20-acre constructed wetland with observatory and boardwalk, dolomite limestone glades that support an abundance of wildflowers, and 1.5 miles of Meramec River border showcasing floodplain forests and gravel bars. The new 4-acre Whitmire Wildflower Garden displays native Missouri wildflowers in a very accessible setting. The area is also home to the restored Bascom Manor House with displays that address the interaction of humans with the natural world over the last 12,000 years. A 12-mile network of trails and 6 miles of service roads offer opportunities for bicycling, jogging or cross-country skiing and provide additional access to the Arboretum's natural features. Finally the Aboretum frequently conducts a wide variety of educational programs for individuals wanting to learn more about Missouri wildlife and operates a Visitor Center that offers books, seeds, maps and interpretive trail guides.

Restrooms – Picnic Areas

Directions: If in St. Louis, Shaw Arboretum is located just 22 miles west from the interchange of I-44 and I-270. Take I-44 toward Gray Summit and take exit 253 to Missouri Highway 100. Follow the signs to the entrance.

For more information, contact:
Shaw Arboretum
P.O. Box 38
Gray Summit, MO 63039
(314) 451-3512

Nature Photography
Tips From the Authors

Taking pictures is an unobtrusive way to record your nature experiences. These tips might give you a few ideas for your next outing:

- The best times of day to take pictures outdoors are early in the day and again at dusk. The light appears much warmer and colors become much richer.

- Try using black-and-white film and photograph "textures." Close-ups of wood grain, ripples formed in mud and other "detail" shots can make for interesting photographs.

- For best results, try a 100 or 200 speed film—400 speed film also works, but is not quite as suited for outdoor photography.

- To get pictures that have "depth," make sure your photograph has both foreground and background. For example, when taking a picture of the river, try to add foreground by including an interesting rock outcropping or tree to balance the photograph.

- Try giving your photographs an unusual composition. Often, we take pictures with the horizon in the exact middle of the picture.

- Try taking a "silhouette" photograph. When the sun is low on the horizon, try using the darkened foreground to "silhouette," or outline, your fishing or hiking buddies.

Sketching Nature
Tips From the Artist

For me, drawing is a natural projection of my appreciation for the outdoors. I like to sit and enjoy watching all of nature move about me. Some paper and a pen or pencil are all that is needed for an entire afternoon of enjoyment and discovery.

What I love about drawing is there's no formula or outline to follow. Let your imagination flow through your pen and you'll be amazed at what you can create!

FYI

A Few Missouri Facts

BLUEBIRD

State Bird
Chosen in 1927

HAWTHORN

State Flower
Chosen in 1923

CRINOID

State Fossil
Chosen in 1989

HONEY BEE

State Insect
Chosen in 1985

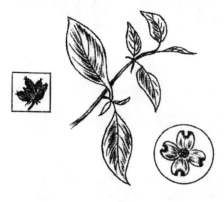

DOGWOOD
State Tree
Chosen in 1955

BLACK WALNUT
State Nut Tree
Chosen in 1990

GALENA
State Mineral
Chosen in 1967

69,674 SQUARE MILES
Missouri is the 19th largest state in total area.

1,772 FEET ABOVE SEA LEVEL
Taum Sauk Mountain is the highest point in the state.

230 FEET ABOVE SEA LEVEL
The lowest point in the state is near Arbyrd.

WINTER NOTES

While using this book as a guide to the Missouri River valley, you may have asked yourself why this book doesn't include information on identifying flora and fauna during the winter? The enjoyment of this diverse area definitely does not end with the coming of colder temperatures; in fact, the winter months often present many new and exciting nature opportunities.

In our effort to present this guide as a primer to the wildlife of this region, we excluded winter identification tips because we wanted to keep this book compact. Perhaps in another edition we will address some of the aspects of nature study that are special to identifying and enjoying winter wildlife but, for now, take along this guidebook no matter what the season—just because leaves fall, flowers disappear, birds migrate and mammals hibernate you shouldn't be kept from discovering the answer to the question "What's that?"

We hope that we have provided you with answers or clues that will help satisfy your curiosity the whole year through.

Glossary

Abdomen – section of body that contains the stomach, intestines and other major internal organs. In insects and spiders, this is the body section that is farthest from the head and attached to the thorax.

Agate – a banded variety of chert. The bands tend to be very delicate and frequently run in parallel.

Alternate – leaves located singly at intervals along stem.

Anther – part of stamen that contains the pollen.

Brachiopod – small marine invertebrate, dominant during Paleozoic and Mesozoic periods. Similar in appearance to tiny mollusk, has two laterally symmetrical valves.

Bract – a small leaf-like structure that is near the flower.

Bryozoa – fairly common small fossil form that is identified by branching or fan-like growth patterns.

Burrow – a home or pathway that is prepared below the surface of the ground, in a tree or other natural feature.

Calcite – essential mineral of limestone (calcium carbonate). Has the chemical formula $CaCO_3$.

Chert – a dull colored, flint-like quartz. Often gray, brown or black and frequently found along with limestone.

Chlorophyll – the photosynthetic pigment present in chloroplasts of green plants that traps energy from sunlight.

Chloroplast – tiny structures within leaf cells of all photosynthetic plants that contain chlorophyll and other photosynthetic pigments.

Chrysalis – the pupa of butterflies and moths.

Clasping – the base of the leaf partly or entirely surrounds the stem.

Colony – a group of individual plants.

Compound Leaf – a leaf divided into 2 or more similar parts called leaflets.

Conifer – non-flowering plant that retains its seeds in cones. Evergreen trees and shrubs are conifers.

Crinoid – branched structured sea creatures that are plant-like—their fossils form Missouri limestone.

Crown – branches and foliage of a tree, the upper portion of a tree.

Deciduous – describes any woody, perennial tree or shrub that sheds its leaves in winter.

Disk – the central tubular flowers in the flower head of the Daisy Family.

Dolomite – limestone rich in magnesium carbonate. Closely resembles calcite. Has the chemical formula $CaMg(CO_3)_2$.

Glossary

Dorsal – uppermost portion, typically the top of the back or the side that faces upward.

Ecosystem – a group of animals, plants and their environment—includes all the abiotic and biotic (living) components of a given are and their interactions.

Elliptical – narrow to rounded ends, widest at the middle.

Evergreen – stays green all winter long.

Female Flower – a flower with pistils, but no stamens.

Filament – part of the stamen that supports the anther.

Frond – the flat, green, food producing part of a fern.

Fruitdots or **Sori** – masses of spore cases or sporangia that are sacks which contains the spores of a fern.

Gill – respiratory organ of aquatic animals. Conducts the gas exchange between the animal and the water in which it lives.

Glade – rocky, open natural clearing free of trees or large shrubs that occurs within a forest.

Gland – organ that produces a chemical substance that is then used outside of the gland. The substance is transported through a duct into the bloodstream, a gland or onto the surface of the skin. In plants, refers to a growth that contains or secretes substances that are by-products of plant metabolism.

Habitat – environment of a specific animal, plant or group of these creatures. Describes a geographic region with uniform climatic conditions.

Head – in plants, a dense cluster of flowers.

Hibernate – to enter into a state of dormancy. Many animals hibernate during the winter when temperatures are significantly cooler and food is scarce.

Hood – curved part of some flowers.

Larva – juvenile or pre-adult form of many animals, morphologically different from an adult. Larva complete a metamorphosis before attaining maturity as adults.

Leaf – expanded blade of a plant that is a flattened appendage of the stem (contains chloroplasts, chlorophyll and other pigments); sites of food production and respiration.

Leaflets – one of the leaf-like segments of a compound leaf.

Limestone – pure limestone is 100 percent calcium carbonate, most often formed from fossil shells and their fragments. There is tremendous variety in the color and texture of different types of limestone.

Loam – soil composed of sand and clay that contains organic matter.

Lobe – part of a flower or leaf that bulges outward.

Male Flower – a flower with stamens, but no pistils.

Marsupial – mammal that has a pouch where undeveloped young are carried and protected until they mature.

Meadow – a region consisting of moist and abundant grasses.

Migratory – describes any animal that embarks on an instinctive round-trip voyage. Migrations often occur during seasonal changes and cover vast distances along well-defined routes.

Mollusk – describes a group of invertebrates that are unsegmented and bilaterally symmetrical.

Mottled – speckled, spotted or blotched. Describes any coloration pattern that includes speckled, spotted or blotched markings.
Native – a plant that is natural to the area.
Opposite or **paired** – leaves located directly across the stem from each other.
Ova – eggs produced by any animal.
Ovary – part of the pistil which contains the structures (ovules) that will become the seeds after fertilization. In animals, the ovary is the egg-producing organ within the female.
Parasite – an animal that lives on or inside another animal (host) at expense to the host.
Pelecypod – a type of bivalved mollusk. Oysters, mussels and clams are living examples of these important fossil contributors.
Petal – part of the flower that is usually brightly colored. Used to attract insects.
Pistil – the female reproductive part of the flower consisting of a stigma, style and ovary.
Pith – spongy tissue in center of the stem and, in some plants, also the roots.
Pollen – the male microspores of seed plants. The wind and insects most often carry out the transfer of pollen from one plant to another.
Predator – any animal that feeds upon other animals.
Prey – any animal that is fed upon by another.
Pupa – the third stage in an insect's development from its larval and adult forms. This is typically (but not always) an immobile stage where the insect completes its metamorphosis.
Pyrite – metallic, brassy yellow, mineral composed of iron sulphide and sulphur. Also called Fool's Gold.
Quartz – composed of silicon dioxide, is an extremely hard mineral with a high luster. Has the chemical formula SiO_2.
Ray – the outer flowers in the flower head of the Daisy Family.
Root – structure that grows out from the stem and anchors a plant into the ground. Functions to transport water and minerals from the soil to the plant and provides support.
Rosette – leaves arranged in a circle at the base of the plant.
Sandstone – rock composed of sand-sized particles, it is an aggregate of small particles that is often held together by silica or carbonate of lime.
Sedimentary – rock formed through the settling of its components through air or water over time—layered rock.
Sepal – the most outer part of the flower, protects the flower when in bud. May be green or colored like the petals.
Sessile – without a stalk.
Shale – rock formed from compressed, layered or laminated clay or mud. Typically has a fine grain.
Slough – a muddy reserve that is often filled with water. A backwater area formed along a river.
Species – a collection or group of organisms whose members may interbreed and produce viable offspring.

Glossary

Spike – a tall cluster of stalkless flowers.

Spore – a single-cell reproductive body. This specialized reproductive cell can develop directly into a new plant.

Spore – simple reproductive bodies of ferns that consists of a single cell. After dispersion spores will become new ferns.

Spur – hollow sac-like or tubular structure on some flowers.

Stalk – the main stem of a plant or flower cluster.

Stamen – the male reproductive part of a flower, consist of an anther and filament.

Stem – main support structure of the plant.

Stigma – a part of a flower that is the top parts of the pistil which receives the pollen.

Style – a part of a flower that is the long structure between the ovary and the stigma.

Sucker – an additional growth that occurs from the root of the parent plant.

Tendril – a slender, coiled organ that attaches to other objects in climbing plants.

Thorax – in vertebrates, this is the body section that contains the heart and lungs. For arthropods and insects this is the region between the head and the abdomen.

Understory – small trees and shrubs that grow under a forest canopy.

Vein (in plants) – vascular tissue in a leaf that forms branching or net-like patterns, they transport liquids and minerals to and from the leaf.

Vent – an opening that serves as the excretory outlet at the end of the digestive tract.

Whorl – group of leaves arranged in circle around the stem.

BIBLIOGRAPHY

Anderson, Paul. *The Reptiles of Missouri.* Columbia: University of Missouri Press, 1965.

Bardach, John. *Downstream: A Natural History of the River.* New York: Harper and Row, 1964.

Behrer, John W. *Native Tree Guide.* Shaw Arboretum, 1987.

Beveridge, Thomas R. *Geologic Wonders and Curiosities of Missouri.* 2nd edition. Revised by Jerry D. Vineyard. Rolla: Missouri Department of Natural Resources, 1990.

Collins, Henry Hill. *Harper and Row's Complete Field Guide to North American Wildlife.* Eastern edition. New York: Harper and Row, 1981.

Denison, Edgar. *Missouri Wildflowers.* 3rd edition. Jefferson City: Missouri Department of Conservation, 1978.

Dirr, Michael A. *Manual of Woody Landscape Plants: Their Identification, Ornamental Characteristics, Culture, Propagation and Uses.* 3rd edition. Champaign: Stipes Publishing, 1983.

Dufur, Brett. *The Complete Katy Trail Guidebook.* 3rd edition. Columbia: Pebble Publishing, 1997.

Eisendrath, Erna R. *Missouri Wildflowers of the St. Louis Area.* St. Louis: Missouri Botanical Garden, 1978.

Elias, Thomas S. *The Complete Trees of North America: Field Guide and Natural History.* New York: Van Nostrand Reinhold, 1980.

Farabee, Gordon. "Fishing Missouri's Big Rivers." *Missouri Conservationist* (August 1995): 11–22.

Ferber, Elizabeth, Bill and Margaret Forbes, Cathy Johnson, Jenna Kinghorn, Mary Kuhner, John Murray, David Rains Wallace and Jan Westmore. *The Walker's Companion.* New York: Time Life Books, 1995.

Fisher, Arden, Joan Murphy and George Rogers, eds. *Missouri Botanical Garden: Know Our Trees.* St. Louis: Missouri Botanical Garden, 1990.

Ganeri, Anita. *Plants.* New York: Franklin Watts, 1992.

Hale, W. G., and J. P. Margham. *The Harper Collins Dictionary of Biology.* Ed. Eugene Ehrlich. New York: HarperCollins, 1991.

Bibliography

Hanenkrat, Frank T. *Wildlife Watcher's Handbook*. New York: Winchester Press, 1977.

Heitzman, Joan E., and Richard J. Heitzman. *Butterflies and Moths of Missouri*. Jefferson City: Missouri Department of Conservation, 1987.

Heumann, Blane. *Vascular Flora Inventory of Katy Trail State Park for Interpretive Planning*. Jefferson City: Missouri Department of Natural Resources, 1994 (unpublished).

Hightshoe, Gary L. *Native Trees, Shrubs, and Vines for Urban and Rural America*. New York: Van Nostrand Reinhold, 1988.

Jackson, Doug, and Debbie Leach. "The Wild Side." *Missouri Conservationist* (April 1996): 30–31.

Johnsgard, Paul A. *Hawks, Eagles, and Falcons of North America*. Washington, D.C.: Smithsonian Institute, 1990.

Johnson, Tom R. "Missouri's Toads and Frogs." *Missouri Conservationist*. Jefferson City: Missouri Conservation Commission, 1982.

Johnson, Tom R. *Missouri's Common Lizards*. Jefferson City: Missouri Department of Conservation, 1985.

Johnson, Tom R. *Snakes of Missouri*. Jefferson City: Missouri Department of Conservation, 1980.

Johnson, Tom R. *The Amphibians and Reptiles of Missouri*. Ed. Kathy Love. Jefferson City: Missouri Department of Conservation, 1987.

Key, James S. *Field Guide to Missouri Ferns*. Jefferson City: Missouri Department of Conservation, 1982.

Kress, Stephen W. *The Audubon Society Handbook for Birders*. New York: Charles Scribner's Sons, 1981.

Ladd, Doug. *Tallgrass Prairie Wildflowers*. Helena: Falcon Press, 1995.

Marx, David S. *The American Book of the Woods*. Cincinatti: Botanic Publishing, 1940.

Milne, Lorus, and Margery Milne. *National Audubon Society Field Guide to North American Insects and Spiders*. New York: Alfred A. Knopf, 1980.

Palmer, Bruce. "Fall Oaks and Hickories." *Missouri Conservationist* (January 1994): 22–23.

Peattie, Donald C. *A Natural History of Trees of Eastern and Central North America*. Boston: Houghton Mifflin, 1950.

Peterson, Roger Tory, and Margaret McKenny. *A Field Guide to Wildflowers: Northeastern and Northcentral America*. Boston: Houghton Mifflin, 1968.

Peterson, Roger Tory. *A Field Guide to the Birds*. Boston: Houghton Mifflin, 1980.

Pflieger, William L. *The Fishes of Missouri*. Jefferson City: Missouri Department of Conservation, 1975.

Phillips, Jan. *Wild Edibles of Missouri*. 1st edition. Jefferson City: Missouri Department of Conservation, 1979.

Pierce, Don. *Exploring Missouri River Country*. Jefferson City: Missouri Department of Natural Resources, Division of Parks and Historic Preservation, n.d.

Richard, J., and Joan E. Heitzman. *Butterflies and Moths of Missouri*. Jefferson City: Missouri Department of Conservation, 1996.

Robbins, Mark B., and David A. Easterla. *Birds of Missouri: Their Distribution and Abundance*. Columbia: University of Missouri Press, 1992.

Schwartz, Charles W., and Elizabeth R. Schwartz. *The Wild Mammals of Missouri*. Columbia: University of Missouri Press, 1981.

Settergren, Carl, and R. E. McDermott. *Trees of Missouri*. Columbia: University of Missouri Press, 1983.

Shosteck, Robert. *Flowers and Plants*. New York: New York Time Book Co., 1974.

Stokes, Donald W. *A Guide to Bird Behavior*. Vol. I. Boston: Little, Brown, 1979.

Taylor, Norman. *A Guide to the Wild Flowers*. Garden City: Garden City, 1928.

Unklesbay, A. G., and Jerry D. Vineyard. *Missouri Geology: Three Billion Year of Volcanoes, Seas, Sediments, and Erosion*. Columbia: University of Missouri Press, 1992.

Wehnes, Rich, and others, "Kids Pitch In." *Streams for the Future* 10.13. Missouri Department of Conservation.

Weidensaul, Scott. *The Birder's Miscellany*. New York: Simon and Schuster, 1991.

Wilson, James D. *An Introduction to Bird Study in Missouri*. Jefferson City: Missouri Department of Conservation, 1979.

Wylie, J. E., and Ramon Gass. *Missouri Trees*. Jefferson City: Missouri Department of Conservation, 1993.

Yatskievych, George and Joanna Turner. *Catalogue of the Flora of Missouri—Monographs in Systematic Botany*. Vol. 37. Missouri Botanical Garden, 1990.

Suggested Readings

The following list of suggested readings has been prepared to help you find out more about the many great natural features of the Missouri River valley. Although each source listed in the bibliography offers a wealth of facts and information, we chose to highlight the following texts because we found them especially valuable. By expanding your reading to include one or more of these works, you will likely go beyond being able to answer "What's that?" and come to understand a significant amount of natural history and lore.

The Reptiles of Missouri
by Paul Anderson

Harper and Row's Complete Field Guide to North American Wildlife
by Henry Hill Collins

Missouri Wildflowers of the St. Louis Area
by Erna R. Eisendrath

Butterflies and Moths of Missouri
by Joan and Richard Heitzman

Field Guide to Missouri Ferns
by James S. Key

Tallgrass Prairie Wildflowers
by Doug Ladd

A Natural History of Trees of Eastern and Central North America
by Donald C. Peattie

The Fishes of Missouri
by William L. Pflieger

Exploring Missouri River Country
by Don Pierce

The Wild Mammals of Missouri
by Charles and Elizabeth Schwartz

Missouri Geology: Three Billion Year of Volcanoes, Seas, Sediments, and Erosion
by A. G. Unklesbay and Jerry D. Vineyard

ADDITIONAL RESOURCES

For free brochures and information on many aspects of Missouri nature, write the Missouri Department of Conservation at P.O. Box 180, Jefferson City, MO 65102-0180. These brochures are a great way to learn about every species out there. They also offer a free map called Outdoor Missouri, which highlights state parks, fishing accesses and state and national forests.

Department of Natural Resources Division of State Parks
P.O. Box 176
Jefferson City, MO 65102
(573) 751-2479 or 1 (800) 334-6946

Division of Tourism
P.O. Box 1055
Jefferson City, MO 65102
(573) 751-4133

For trip planning information
call the "Wake Up to Missouri" hotline:
1 (800) 877-1234.

National Wildlife Federation
1412 16th St. NW
Washington, DC 20036

United States Fish and Wildlife Service
Federal Building
Ft. Snelling
Twin Cities, MN 55111

If you would like to grow Missouri wildflowers near your home, check at a local nursery, or you can order seeds by mail both from companies and also from state agencies. If you want an inexpensive starter-packet of assorted wildflower seeds and instructions to help you start your wildflower garden, send $2 to Pebble Publishing, P.O. Box 431, Columbia, MO 65205. Please include your full name, address and telephone number. Good luck!

WEBSITES YOU SHOULD EXPLORE:

Missouri Conservation Department Website: conservation.state.mo.us
Department of Natural Resources: www.state.mo.us/dnr/dsp/homedesp.htm
Interactive Katy Trail: katytrail.showmestate.com

ZAP! Missouri's Katy Trail State Park
now Accessible from Cyberspace

Parts of the *Katy Trail Guidebook* are now available in a convenient online edition, called the *Interactive Katy Trail*, opening up the trail to 10 million "cyberhikers" worldwide, who surf the Internet for fun and information.

The site was developed by Global Image, Inc., an award-winning producer of sites on the Internet's World-Wide Web, and Pebble Publishing.

The online guide, the first and most complete online rails-to-trails to hit the Internet, includes updates on trail conditions, area day trips and lots of gorgeous color photographs. There are also forums where people can meet, ask questions, and talk about things like hiking, biking and where to find a place to stay.

Thousands of visitors have surfed by the site since its launch in December 1995. The site's designer, Alan Westenbroek, said, "We've received e-mail from people around the world who are planning trips to Missouri to check out the trail. Groups from other states have visited, who want to use the trail as a model for their own Rails-to-Trails projects."

Since the *Interactive Katy Trail* was launched, its innovative, content-packed design has garnered numerous awards, including mentions in *USA Today,* Point Communications' **Top 5 Percent of the Web Award, Editor's Choice in Reader's Digest,** an award from **Gateway Trailnet** in St. Louis, and was ranked as one of **PC Computing's Top 1,001 Internet Sites.** Dufur says he attributes the number of awards to the site's graphics, easy navigation and striking photography.

For people thinking about a vacation or adventure in Missouri this spring, the *Interactive Katy Trail* is a perfect starting point. The *Interactive Katy Trail* is accessible on the Internet's World-Wide Web at: *katytrail.showmestate.com*

REDUCE, REUSE & RECYCLE

In creating this book, many steps were taken to reduce paper waste. Computers now make "paperless" offices a reality. Paper scrap and early drafts of this book were recycled, and the paper stock for this book is 20 percent pre-consumer waste.

About the Authors

Brian Beatte

Brian Beatte is a native of Cape Girardeau, Missouri, and a graduate of Westminster College in Fulton. As a student of life and nature, Brian has completed a thorough course of travel in the United States, Europe, Southeast Asia and South America—always journeying along the paths less traveled. Following his return from National Outdoor Leadership School in Patagonia, Chile, Brian worked out his thoughts exploring the relationship of nature and literature in his senior English thesis entitled "Emerson and Thoreau: Creation of the Wilderness Ethic."

In addition to his love of literature, Brian is presently preparing to attend medical school. He recently finished an extensive program of life sciences coursework and is presently working at Pebble Publishing as an author, editor and researcher. Brian now lives in Rocheport, Missouri, with his girlfriend, Hope and his canine friend, Beckley.

Brett Dufur

Brett Dufur is the author of *The Complete Katy Trail Guidebook, Best of Missouri Hands* and *Exploring Missouri Wine Country.* He is also co-author of *Forgotten Missourians Who Made History.* He is currently working on a book entitled *The River Revisited,* documenting the 1996 Lewis and Clark reenactment comparing the Missouri River of 1804 to the present.

In addition to books, he is the founder, editor and publisher of Pebble Publishing, a publishing house of regional interest books based in Rocheport, Missouri. He has worked at *Costa Rica Guide* magazine, *Missouri Magazine, River Valley Review* and at several newspapers in Arkansas and Missouri, as well as *Constructor de Caminos,* a Latin American trade magazine.

Brett was born in Kansas City, Missouri. He received both his journalism degree and a degree in Latin American Studies from the University of Missouri–Columbia. He spends his off-hours getting tangled up in words, traveling and exploring with his girlfriend, Tawnee, and his dog, Daisy.

About the Illustrator

Maggie Riesenmy

Maggie lives on the east bank of the Missouri River in Boone County where she and her husband, Robert, operate RiverView Traders and WoodWoman ™ Gallery. This is where you'll find them most of the time, busy creating a wide variety of fine art, basketry, furnishings, jewelry, tipis, food, medicinal and culinary herbs, to mention but a few of their endeavors.

When not at home or at work, you'll find her dancing at a Pow Wow, or eating freshly smoked fish in the moonlight, beside a pristine stream.

A Word about Measurements

Most people in the United States use English measurements of inches, feet, yards and miles for distances, and ounces and pounds for weights. Another system of measurements—the metric system—is very popular in the scientific community and is the standard system relied upon by many other nations. A series of conversion formulas are presented below for easy reference:

Conversion: Multiply by:

Linear Measures

inch (in) to centimeter (cm)	2.540
foot (ft) to meter (m)	0.305
mile (mi) to kilometer (km)	1.609

Volume Measures

gallon (gal) to liter (l)	3.785

Dry Weight Measures

ounce (oz) to gram (gm)	28.350
pound (lb) to kilogram (kg)	0.454

Temperature

Fahrenheit ($^\circ$F) to Celsius ($^\circ$C)

$$^\circ C = \frac{^\circ F - 32}{1.8}$$

INDEX

Index

Index

Life List

T he following list includes the all of flora and fauna entries presented in this book. Take time to check off each of the species as you discover them (or, perhaps, rediscover them)—this is a great way to record your nature experiences and keep track of your learning as you explore the Missouri River valley. In addition to the life list presented, we have also included additional space for recording species that are not included in this guide—write them down and drop us a line if you think they should be included in the next edition! The entries have been arranged in alphabetical order for easy reference.

Trees & Shrubs

Basswood
Tilia americana
Black Haw
Viburnum prunifolium
Black Locust
Robinia pseudoacacia
Black Walnut
Juglans nigra
Black Willow
Salix nigra
Blackjack Oak
Quercus marilandica
Bladdernut
Staphylea trifolia
Box Elder
Acer negundo
Bur Oak
Quercus macrocarpa
Butternut
Juglans cinerea
Chinkapin Oak
Quercus muehlenbergii
Cottonwood
Populus deltoides
Flowering Dogwood
Cornus florida
Hackberry
Celtis—several species

Hawthorn
Crataegus pruinosa
Honey Locust
Gleditsia triacanthos
Ohio Buckeye
Aesculus glabra
Osage Orange
Maclura pomifera
Pawpaw
Asimina triloba
Pecan
Carya illinoensis
Persimmon
Diospyros virginiana
Pin Oak
Quercus palustris
Red Cedar
Juniperus virginiana
Red Mulberry
Morus rubra
Red Osier Dogwood
Cornus stolonifera
Redbud
Cercis canadensis
River Birch
Betula nigra
Sandbar Willow
Salix interior
Sassafras
Sassafras albidum

Shadbush
Amelanchier arborer
Shagbark Hickory
Carya ovata
Shingle Oak
Quercus imbricaria
Silver Maple
Acer saccharinum
Spicebush
Lindera benzoin
Sugar Maple
Acer saccharum
Sumac
Rhus glabra
Sycamore
Platanus occidentalis
Wahoo
Euonymus atropurpureus
White Ash
Fraxinus americana
White Oak
Quercus alba
Wild Crab
Pyrus coronaria
Wild Plum
Prunus americana

Flowering Plants

American Feverfew
Parthenium integrifolium
Bellwort
Uvularia grandiflora
Bird's-Foot Violet
Viola pedata
Black-Eyed Susan
Rudbeckia hirta
Bloodroot
Sanguinaria canadensis
Blue Cardinal Flower
Lobelia siphilitica
Bluebells
Mertensia virginica
Blue-Eyed Mary
Collinsia verna
Bouncing Bet
Saponaria officinalis

Brown-Eyed Susan
Rudbeckia triloba
Bull Thistle
Cirsium vulgare
Butterfly Weed
Asclepias tuberosa
Common Chickory
Cichorium intybus
Common Cinquefoil
Potentilla simplex
Common Dayflower
Commelina communis
Common Ground Cherry
Physalis longifolia
Common Milkweed
Asclepias syriaca
Common Smartweed
Polygonum pensylvanicum
Common Sunflower
Helianthus annuus
Common Violet
Viola sororia
Compass Plant
Silphium laciniatum
Crown Vetch
Securigera varia
(formerly *Coronilla varia*)
Cup Plant
Silphium perfoliatum
Dutchman's Breeches
Dicentra cucullaria
Dwarf Larkspur
Delphinium tricorne
Eastern Prickly Pear Cactus
Opuntia humifusa (formerly *Opuntia compressa*)
False Rue Anemone
Isopyrum biternatum
Flowering Spurge
Euphorbia corollata
Goat's Beard
Aruncus dioicus
Green-Stemmed Joe-Pye Weed
Eupatorium purpureum
Ground Ivy
Glechoma hederacea
Hairy Vetch
Vicia villosa
Harbinger Of Spring
Erigenia bulbosa

Life List

Hedge Parsley
Torilis nodosa
Henbit
Lamium amplexicaule
Ironweed
Vernonia baldwinii
Jack-In-The-Pulpit
Arisaema triphyllum
Jacob's Ladder
Polemonium reptans
Jerusalem Artichoke
Helianthus tuberosus
Jimsonweed
Datura stramonium
Johnny-Jump-Up
Viola rafinesquii
Lance-Leaved Loosestrife
Lysimachia lanceolata
Lead Plant
Amorpha canescens
Mad-Dog Skullcap
Scutellaria lateriflora
May Apple
Podophyllum peltatum
Mullein
Verbascum thapsus
Ohio Spiderwort
Tradescantia ohiensis
Orange Day Lily
Hemerocallis fulva
Orange Puccoon
Lithospermun canescens
Ox-Eye Daisy
Leucanthemum vulgare (formerly
Chrysanthemum leucanthemum)
Pale Cordyalis
Corydalis flavula
Pale-Purple Coneflower
Echinacea pallida
Partridge Pea
Chamaecrista fasciculata (formerly
Cassia fasciculata)
Pasture Rose
Rosa carolina
Philadelphia Fleabane
Erigeron philadelphicus
Poison Hemlock
Conium maculatum
Pokeweed
Phytolacca americana

Prairie Blue-Eyed Grass
Sisyrinchium campestre
Prairie Rose
Rosa setigera
Pussy's Toes
Antennaria plantaginifolia
Queen Anne's Lace
Daucus carota
Red Clover
Trifolium pratense
Rose Vervain
Glandularia candensis (formerly
Verbena candensis)
Rough Blazing Star
Liatris aspera
Rue Anemone
Anemonella thalictroides
Sensitive Brier
Schrankia nuttallii
Sheep Sorrel
Rumex acetosella
Shepard's Purse
Capsella bursa-pastoris
Shooting Star
Dodecatheon meadia
Showy Goldenrod
Solidago speciosa
Small Bluets
Hedyotis crassifolia (formerly
Houstionia pusilla)
Smooth Beard–Tongue
Penstemon digitalis
Solomon's Seal
Polygonatum biflorum
Spotted St. John's-Wort
Hypericum punctatum
Spotted Touch-Me-Not
Impatiens capensis
Spring Beauty
Claytonia virginica
Star-Of-Bethlehem
Ornithogalum umbellatum
Swamp Buttercup
Ranunculus hispidus
Toothwort
Cardamine concatenata
Velvet Leaf
Abutilon theophrasti
Wake Robin Trillium
Trillium sessile

Water Hemlock
Cicuta maculata
Watercress
Rorippa nasturtium-aquaticum
(formerly *Nasturtium officinale*)
White Anemone
Anemone canadensis
White Clover
Trifolium repens
White Heather Aster
Aster pilosus
White Snakeroot
Eupatorium rugosum
White Sweet Clover
Melilotus albus
White Trout Lily
Erythronium albidum
White Wild Indigo
Baptisia alba (formerly *Baptisia leucantha*)
Wild Bergamont
Monarda fistulosa
Wild Columbine
Aquilegia canadensis
Wild Garlic
Allium canadenses
Wild Geranium
Geranium maculatum
Wild Ginger
Asarum canadense
Wild Hyacinth
Camassia scilloides
Wild Lettuce
Lactuca canadensis
Wild Parsnip
Pastinaca sativa
Wild Senna
Senna marilandica (formerly *Cassia marilandica*)
Wild Strawberry
Fragaria virginiana
Wild Sweet William
Phlox divaricata
Winged Loosestrife
Lythrum alatum
Wood Betony
Pedicularis canadensis
Yarrow
Achillea millefolium

Yellow Goat's Beard
Tragopogon dubius
Yellow Rocket
Barbarea vulgaris
Yellow Star Grass
Hypoxis hirsuta
Yellow Violet
Viola pubescens (formerly *Viola pensylvanica*)

VINES, CANES & RUSHES

American Bittersweet
Celastrus scandens
Black Raspberry
Rubus occidentalis
Blackberry
Rubus pensilvanicus
Blue Morning Glory
Ipomoea hederacea
Bristly Greenbrier
Smilax hispida
Common Cat-Tail
Typha latifolia
Dewberry
Rubus flagellaris
Field Bindweed
Convolvulus arvensis
Graybark Grape
Vitis cinerea
Japanese Honeysuckle
Lonicera japonica
Missouri Gooseberry
Ribes missouriense
Multiflora Rose
Rosa multiflora
Poison Ivy
Toxicodendron radicans (formerly *Rhus radicans*)
Trumpet Creeper
Campsis radicans
Virginia Creeper
Parthenocissus quinquefolia
Wild Potato Vine
Ipomoea pandurata

Plants with Stickers, Burs, Seeds or Other Parts That Stick You

Bedstraw
Galium aparine
Cocklebur
Xanthium spinosum
Sticktights
Biden frondosa
Stinging Nettle
Laportea canadensis
Tick Trefoil
Desmodium glutinosum

Prairie Grasses

Big Blue Stem
Andropogon gerardit
Little Blue Stem
Andropogon scoparius

Ferns

Christmas Fern
Polystichum acrostichoides
Fragile Fern
Cystopteris protrusa
Horsetails
Equisetum hyemale
Northern Maidenhair Fern
Adiantum pedatum
Purple Cliff Brake
Pellaea atropurpurea
Rattlesnake Fern
Botrychium virginianum
Sensitive Fern
Onoclea sensibilis
Walking Fern
Asplenium rhizophyllum

Birds

American Crow
Corvus brachyrhynchos
Bald Eagle
Haliaeetus leucocephalus
Barn Swallow
Hirundo rustica
Barred Owl
Strix varia
Black Capped Chickadee
Parus atricapillus
Blue Jay
Cyanocitta cristata
Bluebird
Sialia sialis
Blue-Gray Gnatcatcher
Polioptila caerulea
Blue-Winged Teal
Anas discors
Brown Thrasher
Toxostoma rufum
Cardinal
Cardinalis cardinalis
Carolina Wren
Thryothorus ludovicianus
Cedar Waxwing
Bombycilla cedrorum
Chimney Swift
Chaetura pelagica
Common Grackle
Quiscalus quiscula
Cowbird
Molothrus ater
Dark-Eyed Junco
Junco hyemalis
Double-Crested Cormorant
Phalacrocorax auritus
Downy Woodpecker
Picoides pubescens
Eastern Kingbird
Tyrannus tyrannus
Eastern Meadowlark
Sturnelia magna
Eastern Phoebe
Sayornis phoebe
Giant Canada Goose
Branta canadensis

Goldfinch
Carduelis tristis
Great Blue Heron
Ardea herodias
Great Egret
Casmerodius albus
Green Heron
Butorides striatus
Horned Lark
Eremophila alpestris
House Sparrow
Passer domesticus
House Wren
Troglodytes aedon
Indigo Bunting
Passerina cyanea
Kestrel
Falco sparverius
Killdeer
Charadrius vociferus
Kingfisher
Ceryle alcyon
Mallard
Anas platyrhynchos
Mourning Dove
Zenaida macroura
Northern Bob White
Colinus virginianus
Northern Flicker
Colaptes auratus
Northern Mockingbird
Mimus polyglotto
Northern Oriole
Icterus galbula
Pileated Woodpecker
Dryocopus pileatus
Purple Martin
Progne subis
Red-Bellied Woodpecker
Melanerpes carolinus
Red-Headed Woodpecker
Melanerpes erthrocephalus
Red-Tailed Hawk
Buteo jamaicensis
Red-Winged Blackbird
Agelaius phoeniceus
Robin
Turdus migratorius
Rock Dove or Pigeon
Columba livia

Rose-Breasted Grosbeak
Pheucticus ludovicianus
Ruby-Throated Hummingbird
Archilochus colubris
Song Sparrow
Melospiza melodia
Starling
Sturnus vulgaris
Tufted Titmouse
Parus bicolor
Turkey Vulture
Cathartes aura
White Pelican
Pelecanus erythrorhychos
White-Breasted Nuthatch
Sitta carolinensis
Wild Turkey
Meleagris gallopavo
Wood Duck
Aix sponsa
Yellow Warbler
Dendroica petechia

Butterflies

Blues and Common Brown Hairstreak
Brush-Footed Butterflies
Monarch Butterflies
Skippers
Sulphurs And Whites
Swallowtails

Insects
& Insect Relatives

Ants
Black Widow
Brown Recluse
Bumble Bees
Chiggers
Cicadas
Daddy Longlegs
Damselflies

Life List

Insects & Insect Relatives

(CONTINUED)

Dragonflies
Grasshoppers
Ground Beetles
Honey Bees
Horseflies
Jumping Spiders
Ladybugs
Midges
Mosquitoes
No-See-Ums
Sweat Bees
Ticks
Velvet Mites
Walking Sticks
Wasps
Water Striders
Whirligig Beetles
Wolf Spiders

Mammals

Bat
  Myotis—several species
Beaver
  Castor canadensis
Bobcat
  Lynx rufus
Chipmunk
  Tamias striatus
Cottontail Rabbit
  Sylvilagus floridanus
Coyote
  Canis latrans
Deer Mouse
  Peromyscus maniculatus
Fox Squirrel
  Sciurus niger
Gray Fox
  Urocyon cinereoargenteus
Gray Squirrel
  Sciurus carolinensis
Mink
  Mustela vison
Mole
  Scalopus aquaticus
Muskrat
  Ondatra zibethicus
Opossum
  Didelphis virginiana
Raccoon
  Procyon lotor
Rat
  Rattus norvegicus
Red Fox
  Vulpes vulpes
River Otter
  Lontica canadensis
Shrew
  Blarina brevicauda
Striped Skunk
  Mephitis mephites
Weasel
  Mustela frenata
White-Tailed Deer
  Odocoileus virginianus
Woodchuck or Groundhog
  Marmota monax

Reptiles & Amphibians

Black or Rat Snake
  Elaphe obsoleta obsoleta
Bullsnake
  Pituophis melanoleucus sayi
Copperhead
  Agkistrodon contortrix phaeogaster
Garter Snake
  Thamnophis sirtalis sirtalis
Hognose Snake
  Heterodon platyrhinos
Kingsnake
  Lampropeltis calligaster calligaster
Red Milk Snake
  Lampropeltis getulus holbrooki
Ringneck Snake
  Diadophis punctatus arnyi

Speckled Snake
Lampropeltis getulus holbrooki
Timber Rattlesnake
Crotalus horridus
Water Snake
Nerodia sipedon sipedon

SALAMANDERS

Spotted Salamander
Ambystoma maculatum

LIZARDS

Blue-Tailed Skink
Eumeces fasciatus
Fence Lizard
Sceloporus undulatus hyacinthinus

FISH

Black Bullhead
Ictalurus melas
Black Crappie
Pomoxis nigromaculatus
Blue Catfish
Ictalurus furcatus
Bluegill
Lepomis macrochirus
Carp
Cyprinus carpio
Channel Catfish
Ictalurus punctatus
Flathead Catfish
Pylodictis olivaris
Freshwater Drum
Aplodinotus grunniens
Largemouth Bass
Micropterus salmoides
Sauger
Stizostedion canadense
Walleye
Stizostedion vitreum
White Bass
Morone chrysops
White Crappie
Pomoxis annularis
Yellow Bullhead
Ictalurus natalis

TURTLES

Box Turtle
Terrapene carolina triunguis
Map Turtle
Graptemy pseudogeographica
Painted Turtle
Chrysemys picta belli
Red-Eared Slider
Chrysemy scripta elegans
Snapping Turtle
Chelydra serpentina serpentina
Softshell Turtle
Trionyx muticus muticus

FROGS & TOADS

American Toad
Bufo americanus americanus
Bullfrog
Rana catesbeiana
Gray Treefrog
Hyla chrysoscelis and *Hyla versicolor*
Plains Leopard Frog
Rana blairi
Southern Leopard Frog
Rana sphenocephala
Spring Peeper
Hyla crucifer crucifer

Notes & Sketches

Notes & Sketches

Notes & Sketches

Notes & Sketches

Notes & Sketches

Notes & Sketches

Notes & Sketches

Notes & Sketches

Notes & Sketches

— The Show Me Missouri Series —

99 Fun Things to Do in Columbia & Boone County
Guide to hidden highlights, galleries, museums, towns, people and history in Columbia, Rocheport, Centralia and Boone County. Most trips are free or under $10. Includes maps and photos. 168 pages. By Pamela Watson. $12.95. ISBN: 0-9646625-2-3

A to Z Missouri—A dictionary-style book of Missouri place name origins
Abo to Zwanzig! Includes history, pronunciations, population, county, post office dates and more. 220 pages. By Margot Ford McMillen. $14.95. ISBN: 0-9646625-4-X

The Complete Katy Trail Guidebook—America's longest Rails-to-Trails Project
The definitive guide to services, towns, people, places and history along Missouri's 200-mile Katy Trail. This third edition covers the cross-state hiking and biking trail from Clinton to St. Charles. Includes maps, 80 photos and more. 168 pages. By Brett Dufur. $14.95. ISBN: 0-9646625-0-7

Daytrip Missouri—The tour guide standard for Missouri
Includes annual events, travel tips, 60 photos and 20 maps. 224 pages. By Lee N. Godley and Patricia Murphy O'Rourke. $14.95. ISBN: 0-9651340-0-8

Exploring Missouri Wine Country
This guidebook profiles wineries, including how to get there, their histories, wine tips, home-brew recipes, dictionary of wine terms and more. Also lists nearby bed & break-fasts, services and state parks. 192 pages. By Brett Dufur. $14.95. ISBN: 0-9646625-6-6

Forgotten Missourians Who Made History
A book of short stories and humorous comic-style illustrations of more than 35 Missourians who made a contribution to the state or nation yet are largely forgotten by subsequent generations. Compiled by Jim Borwick and Brett Dufur. $14.95. ISBN: 0-9646625-8-2

Missouri Ghosts—Spirits, Haunts & Related Lore
A lifetime's collection of spirits, haunts and folklore from around the state. This intriguing book highlights more than a century of Missouri's most spine-chilling and unexplainable phenomena. By Joan Gilbert. 230 pages. $14.95

River Rat's Guide to Missouri River Folklore and History
A Missouri River classic, documented bend by bend by river rat and historian Cecil Griffith. First published in 1974. Reissued with new maps and more. 144 pages. $14.95

The River Revisited—Reflections In the Wake of Lewis and Clark
Includes excerpts from the original voyage, as well as modern-day commentary from the 200 years since Lewis and Clark. Includes pull-out map of the Missouri River, 50 photos and journals from a modern-day crew of reenactors. 224 pages. By Brett Dufur. $16.95. ISBN: 0-9646625-9-0

Wit & Wisdom of Missouri's Country Editors
More than 600 pithy sayings from pioneer Missouri papers. Many of these quotes and quips date to the 19th century yet remain timely for today's readers. Richly illustrated and fully indexed to help you find that perfect quote. 168 pages. By William Taft. $14.95

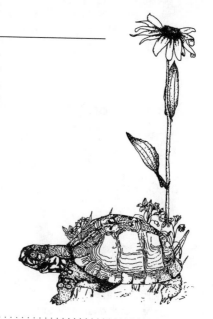

Show Me Missouri books are available at many local bookstores. They can also be ordered directly from the publisher, using this form, or ordered by phone, fax or over the Internet.

Pebble Publishing also distributes 100 other books of regional interest, rails-to-trails, Missouri history, heritage, nature, recreation and more. These are available through our online bookstore and mail-order catalog.

Visit our online bookstore, *Trailside Books,* on the Internet at Trailsidebooks.com. If you would like to receive our free catalog, please fill out and mail the form on this page.

Pebble Publishing

P.O. Box 431 ❖ Columbia, MO 65205-0431
1 (800) 576-7322 ❖ Fax: (573) 698-3108

Quantity	*Book Title*	*x Unit Price = Total*

Mo. residents add 6.975% sales tax = _____
Shipping ($2 first book, $1 each additional book) x = _____
Total = _____

☐ $2 enclosed for wildflower seed packet (book order not required)

Name:_____

Email Address:_____

Address:_____ Apt._____

City, State, Zip _____

Phone: (____) _____

Credit Card # _____

Expiration Date _____/_____/_____   Please send catalog _____

Visit *Trailside Books* online at Trailsidebooks.com

Praise for Brett Dufur's previous work
The Complete Katy Trail Guidebook

and . . .

Exploring Missouri Wine Country

"Dufur seems to have picked up a few pointers from William Least Heat Moon, whose *Blue Highways* and *PrairyErth* achieve depth through historical anecdotes and colorful character descriptions . . . For day-trippers as well as long-distance bikers and hikers, the *Katy Trail Guidebook* is a worthwhile investment. They will do well to make room for it in an easily accessible pocket."
— *Christopher Ryan*
Ozark Sierran

"Where most guidebook authors finish, Dufur is just getting warmed up. . . . This book contains fun facts not even a history teacher would know."
— *Chuck MacDonald*
St. Louis Times

"Dufur, a reporter by schooling, has an eye for stories. . . . And after a long jaunt through Latin America, he knows the value of a good guidebook. "
— *Lisa Groshong*
Columbia Daily Tribune